KILLED IN ACTION

The life and times of SP4 Stephen H. Warner, draftee, journalist and anti-war activist

Arthur J. Amchan

Amchan Publications
7010 Westbury Rd.
McLean, VA 22101

Email: Nmiles@starpower.net

KILLED IN ACTION

The Life and Times of SP4 Stephen H. Warner, draftee, journalist and anti-war activist

By Arthur J. Amchan

Published by:

Amchan Publications
7010 Westbury Rd.
McLean, Virginia 22101

Library of Congress Control Number: 2003105606
ISBN: 0-9617132-4-0

Table of Contents

War, horrid war, waged for its own sake is ignoble, brutal; but when waged in defense of convictions which deserve to prevail, then indeed may war be glorified and sanctified by the suffering and the lives of its victims.

> Norwood P. Hallowell, formerly Lieutenant Colonel, 55th Massachusetts Volunteer Infantry, from his speech, *The Meaning of Memorial Day*, May 30, 1896 to the graduating class of Harvard College.

"Sentimental Jingoism"

By this we would charitably characterize the address delivered by Judge Oliver Wendell Holmes at Sanders Theatre, Cambridge on Memorial Day...

Its theme was "The Soldier's Faith" and its object to glorify war and the war spirit. The young men who listened to it...were admonished that 'war is the business of youth and early middle age' and were encouraged to pity the moralists and philanthropists who declare that war is wicked, foolish, and soon to disappear.

***

As we take notice above, a judge of the Massachusetts Supreme Court has just printed an address to young men in favor of war--that is, of killing people and destroying their property--on the ground that if you put it off too long, your character runs down and you get too fond of money.

> *The Nation*, Editorial, Vol. 61, p. 440, December 19, 1895.

The Cubans...are not worth fighting for, but, of course everybody knows that. However, we have not forgotten the Maine and besides, war is the natural state of mankind.

> Major Matthew Batson, 9th U.S. Cavalry Regiment, quoted in David Trask, *The War With Spain in 1898*, at page 210

In the last days of January 1971 American forces in Vietnam began their most ambitious operation since the Cambodian invasion nine months earlier. Dewey Canyon II, or Lam Son 719, as it was called by the South Vietnamese, was destined to be the last major U.S. ground offensive of the war. American bombers and helicopters attacked North Vietnamese forces in Laos to assist the South Vietnamese Army (ARVN) in trying to cut Communist supply lines along the Ho Chi Minh trail. At the same time, large numbers of American ground troops moved into the northwestern portions of South Vietnam's Quang Tri Province to provide security and logistical support for the ARVN troops on the other side of the border.

The war that the American soldier was fighting in 1971 was a very different war from the one it had been prior to 1968. No longer did many Americans have enthusiasm for the Vietnam War. Fewer and fewer people in the U.S. or soldiers in Southeast Asia believed that the sacrifices made in the war would save South Vietnam. Many, if not most, Americans now believed that the War served no purpose at all. Nevertheless, many Americans were still uneasy about the prospect of abandoning this costly effort.

Although the Laos offensive rekindled the waning interest in the conflict in the United States, war news did not, as it had in the past, eclipse other stories. The lead article in *The New York Times* on February 15, 1971, for example, was not about the Vietnam War but rather concerned the agreement by 23 western oil companies to pay $10 billion to six Persian Gulf States to stabilize the oil industry. Another front-page story reported that Egyptian President Anwar Sadat would be willing to reopen the Suez Canal if Israeli forces withdrew eastward into the Sinai Peninsula. Two and a half years later, Sadat tried to recapture the Sinai by arms. Seven years later he signed a peace treaty with Israel and ten years later he was assassinated for his trouble.

The Times also reported on page one the end of the first 100 days of the democratically elected Marxist government of Salvador Allende in Chile. Allende was to be overthrown by a military coup and murdered in 1973. The degree of American active and/or tacit support for the coup, which was followed by a brutal military dictatorship that endured until 1989, remains one of the many controversies surrounding the presidency of Richard Nixon.

The newspaper also accorded front-page coverage to the announcement of a new five-year economic plan by the Soviet leader Leonid Brezhnev. Less attention was given to a strike by workers in Lodz, Poland, which was part of a series of events leading to the destruction of European Communism.

While *The Times* gave front-page coverage to the Vietnam War, the war news did not engender the intense reaction that it had in 1968, 1969 and during the Cambodian invasion of May and June 1970. Indeed, on February 15, 1971, *The Washington Post* ran columns by Stanley Karnow and Marquis Childs, commenting on the lack of protest activity on the nations' campuses and contrasting this to the upheavals of just nine months before.[1] By and large, most Americans went about their lives fairly oblivious to the fact that American soldiers were still fighting and dying in Southeast Asia. The implementation of a draft lottery, declining draft calls, relatively fewer casualties and a reduction in the number of American troops in Vietnam had for the most part returned the war to the back burner in the minds of most Americans.

Even in Vietnam, Lam Son 719 had little impact on those American soldiers not directly involved in the operation. At the U.S. Forces' headquarters complex at Tan Son Nhut Air Force Base near Saigon, rear echelon soldiers went swimming in a large modern pool and played basketball and racquetball in a modern gymnasium facility while other American soldiers were risking their lives a few hundred miles to the North.

On February 16, 1971, *The Times* reported the 6th scheduled reduction in the number of American troops in Vietnam. Troop levels had declined to 332,900 from a peak of approximately 540,000 in 1969. By May 1, 1971, the number of U.S. servicemen in Vietnam would be down to 284,000. However, there was plenty of action for those American soldiers still "in country." Although the frequency and intensity of combat in South Vietnam had decreased dramatically since 1968 and 1969, an average of a dozen U.S. servicemen had been killed in combat everyday during calendar year 1970; an average of five more died every day in Vietnam from non-hostile causes.[2] In February 1971, helicopter crews were fighting and dying in Laos. There were also plenty of well-armed North Vietnamese soldiers lurking about throughout in the hills and jungles of South Vietnam.

Among the ground troops involved in Dewey Canyon II were soldiers from A Company of the 7th Engineer battalion. These engineers were building a new road through dense vegetation and over steep hills, to run parallel to route 9, the main road from the Khe Sanh base camp to the Laotian border. Infantrymen from the First Brigade of the 5th Mechanized Infantry Division provided security for the construction crews.

On February 14, a North Vietnamese soldier hit one of the engineers' armored personnel carriers (APC) with a rocket-propelled grenade. The grenade exploded on the machine gun splinter shield spraying shrapnel into the crew. Four soldiers were killed or died of their wounds, one other was wounded and survived, and a sixth managed to escape injury.[3] Elsewhere in South Vietnam, three other American soldiers died the same day. The deaths on the APC were reported, if at all, by *The Times*, albeit inaccurately, on February 17, in conjunction with a reported clash between American troops and Communist forces near route 9:

---

[1] *The Post* devoted even less space to the Vietnam War than *The Times*, reporting primarily on the mistaken attack by American planes on a CIA outpost in Laos.
[2] The annual totals for 1970 were: 4,221 KIA (killed in action); 1,844 non-hostile deaths; total 6,065-- compared with 5,008 KIA in 1966; 9,378 KIA in 1967; 14,594 KIA in 1968, 9,414 KIA in 1969; 1,380 KIA in 1971 and 300 KIA in 1972.
[3] May 14, 2002 interview with Lee McCain, a squad leader in A company, who was in command of another APC on February 14, 1971; 2002 emails from Alfonso Varela, another member of A company.

Three other Americans were killed and six wounded in the same area when a patrol was ambushed 10 miles from Khe Sanh...

The scant attention to the incident underscores the fact that the death of an individual soldier, particularly one of lower rank, has little significance to anyone other than his family and friends. The German Pacifist, Eric Marie Remarque, made this point in his novel of World War I, "All Quiet on the Western Front"[More literally translated as "No News in the West"]. Remarque's title is the German High Command's fictional communiqué for the day his protagonist died. The generals did not even notice the death of Remarque's hero.

Three of the Americans who died in Quang Tri on February 14, 1971 were fairly typical of the over 58,000 Americans killed in Vietnam between 1959 and 1972. Ronald Calvin Ruff, from Notasulga, Alabama, was a combat engineer, who had just turned 20 and had been in Vietnam since June 1970. Richard Dean Covert was also a combat engineer. He was 19 ½ years old, from Pleasanton, California, and had only been in Vietnam for two months, after completing a non-commissioned officer's school at Fort Leonard Wood, Missouri. Douglas Lee Horn, a 20-year old from Kansas City, Missouri, was an infantryman, who had been in Vietnam for four months, at least some it as a combat medic.

The fourth soldier killed, however, was very atypical. Stephen Henry Warner was an Army Public Information Specialist from Skillman, New Jersey. He was a week shy of his twenty-fifth birthday and only a few weeks away from returning home after 11 months in Vietnam. Steve Warner had completed his first year at Yale Law School, the most selective law school in the United States. A 1968 magna cum laude graduate of Gettysburg College, Steve had been active in the anti-war movement in college and was bitterly opposed to U.S. involvement in the Vietnam War.

The vast majority of American soldiers killed in Vietnam had absolutely no control over the circumstances that led to their deaths. Specialist Four (SP4)[4] Stephen Warner, however, did not have to be in Quang Tri Province on the day he died. In the normal course of events, he would have been at the Army's headquarters post at Long Binh, just north of Saigon, preparing for his return to the United States, two weeks hence. However, he begged his superiors for permission to cover operations in Quang Tri and had even given up a week's vacation (R & R) in Hong Kong and a three-week early termination of his Vietnam tour (called a "drop" by the troops) to do so.

Stephen Warner was different from most of the soldiers in Vietnam in other respects as well. Most GIs were assigned to one unit and had little information as to what

---

[4] Army enlisted ranks during Vietnam ranged from E-1 (Private) to E-9 (Sergeant Major). Once past E-3 (Private First Class), your designation depended on whether you had command responsibility over other soldiers. An E-4 who had such responsibilities was a Corporal; an E-4, who didn't was a Specialist (Spec) 4. E-5s were either Sergeants or Specialist 5s. Generally, those enlisted men above an E-5 were Sergeants; E-6, Staff Sergeant (SSG); E-7, Sergeant First Class (SFC); E-8 Master Sergeant (MSG). Normally, only career enlisted soldiers obtained rank above an E-5. Above the enlisted men in rank, but below the commissioned officers were warrant officers, many of which were helicopter pilots.

other soldiers in other units and in other areas of South Vietnam were doing. Steve visited many units in many different parts of Vietnam over the course of eleven months. He also recorded what he saw and how he reacted to what he observed. Steve Warner so passionately believed that the United States should not have been fighting the Vietnam War that he seriously considered refusing to comply with orders to report there. However, once he got to Vietnam and was assigned duty as an army journalist, he repeatedly volunteered to go out in the field to report on the lives of the combat soldiers. Throughout his tour in Vietnam, Steve sent material on the war to the library at Gettysburg College and planned to write a book about his experiences in the war.[5]

I intend to help Steve Warner fulfill that ambition. However, this book is also the story of a generation of American males, including this author, who found themselves confronted by the quandary created by the Vietnam War. I decided to undertake this book when I accidentally came across Gettysburg College's on-line exhibit on Steve Warner (whom I did not know).[6] I was struck by how similar he was to me.

We were born six days apart and were both drafted out of law school in June 1969. I started basic training at Fort Dix, New Jersey, three weeks after Steve and arrived in Vietnam three weeks after he started his tour. I returned home one month after he was killed. We were both opposed to further American participation in the Vietnam War, although his opposition came earlier and I believe was more principled. Due to the paucity of information about Steve's experiences in basic training, I have filled this gap with my own experiences, which I assume were very similar since they occurred at the same time and at the same place.[7] I have also used my letters home, fortunately saved by my parents, to corroborate and, in some cases, to elucidate some of the observations made by Steve Warner in his letters home from Vietnam during 1970 and 1971.

Steve and I both were given relatively safe assignments in Vietnam; Steve at Long Binh, myself in Saigon. When I first came across the Gettysburg website, the first thing I wanted to know was how a Yale Law Student managed to get himself killed in Vietnam in 1971--because I suspected Steve really had to tempt fate to do so. As the reader will see, Stephen Warner sacrificed his personal security in order to make his year in Vietnam meaningful. I also believe he exposed himself to risks that many would deem unnecessary to atone for his good fortune in getting a safe assignment due to his education. I'm unsure as to whether he fully appreciated the potential danger in his last

---

[5] Steve also left the proceeds of his GI insurance policy to Gettysburg College to support two projects. One was for the College Library to fund the purchase of books on Asia and to maintain the Warner Collection. The other was "to create an atmosphere of intellectual excitement, doubt and challenge at the College." November 11, 2002 letter from Professor Emeritus Roger Stemen to the author.

[6] The website is found at www.gettysburg.edu/Library/Special Collections. It contains excerpts from some of Steve's letters and a selection of his photographs.

[7] Steve Warner's papers at Gettysburg College contain virtually no references or information about his basic training experience. I wrote his mother, asking if she had a "cycle book," which was similar to a high school yearbook. At Fort Dix in 1969, every basic trainee could have purchased one. Mrs. Warner was unaware that such a book existed. The "cycle books" contained the name and picture of each person in a basic training company. If I had one for Steve Warner's company, I might have been able to locate other soldiers from his basic training company.

assignment, but it is clear that he wanted to experience combat before he returned home. I had no such desire.

One of Steve's closest friends in Vietnam, Sherman Carlson, has shared with me his impression of Steve's motives and his appreciation of danger:

Shortly after he arrived, I was struck by his desire to go out in the field and do his hometown newspaper clips of the guys he met. By that time in the war, most guys had little desire to die for the cause [--] by that time there wasn't one....To begin with, Steve didn't want to carry a firearm, but I think he came to a different conclusion once out in the field (although I don't think he envisioned using it). I believe he had a mission to witness first hand what was going on and a desire (to the degree possible) to tell the story of the grunt in the field....I'm sure Steve struggled with the swimming pools, air conditioned office, restaurant, etc., back at Long Binh, with what he saw in the field. He wanted to give them [the field troops] one snapshot of attention to the folks back home....

In 1970, the war gave you a false sense of security, most especially in the major cities and base camps. Rockets were few, and only occasionally did you see a dead body...but, I often sensed that there was greater danger than Steve realized.[8]

It is impossible to know for certain what motivated Steve to take the chances he took. However, the contrast between one's own situation and the lot of the field soldier is something that troubled many young men in the rear, particularly those who opposed the war and had no desire to be in Vietnam. At some level, most of us realized that many of the young men actually doing the fighting and dying, particularly in the last stages of the war, had no greater desire to be in Vietnam than we did. Although, a far greater portion of our generation missed the Vietnam experience altogether, many of us were bothered by the contrast--even though we had no desire to trade places with the men in the field (one could always have volunteered for combat duty).

On August 23, 1970, I wrote the following in a letter to my parents, explaining why I had written a bitter letter about the war to the editor of *The New York Times*.[9]

It may be that I have acquired a fixation on this subject--but last night I started getting angry about it again--so I wrote the letter. What brought it on was that last night I went to the MACV[10] gym at Tan Son Nhut. I played paddleball (like handball) with some of the junior officers I work with, played a little basketball, took a shower, went to a movie and waited for the bus. While waiting for the bus I was watching some guys playing tennis and the lifeguards cleaning the swimming pool.

---

[8] Email to author May 24, 2002.
[9] Printed in *The Times* on September 1, 1970.
[10] Military Assistance Command Vietnam, the headquarters of the U.S. military located at Tan Son Nhut Air Force Base on the outskirts of Saigon.

I thought, Christ, this can't be Vietnam; this looks like a damn country club. The guys who play here will go home and tell everybody what an important job we are doing over here when they have seen no more of the war than I have. Meanwhile, there are 80,000 guys, mostly draftees, walking around the boondocks who haven't bathed in three months [and] who will go home and probably get busted for smoking pot (if they ever go home).

What bothered me was essentially what bothered Steve Warner. However, as the reader will see, he had a rather unique way of dealing with his dilemma and he died in Vietnam as a result.

Stephen Henry Warner was born on February 21, 1946. He grew up in Skillman, New Jersey, and attended high school in Princeton. His father, Harold J. Warner, was a patent attorney at Johnson & Johnson, the pharmaceutical company, and also served as a municipal judge in New Jersey. Harold Warner served in the Army Air Corps during World War II. After being sent to the Massachusetts Institute of Technology to study meteorology for one year, Harold was assigned to the China/Burma/India Theater. There he spent two years forecasting weather for military flights over the Himalayas between China and India. Mr. Warner was not a stranger to this area. He was born in Bombay and lived in India until he was 12. His father, Steve's paternal grandfather, was a missionary in India, where he built schools for orphan girls. Both of Steve's grandfathers were clergymen.

The Warner household also included his mother, Esther Warner, and his sister Victoria, three years his junior, and his maternal grandfather. While Steve was in college, Esther Warner went to work as a reference librarian at the Princeton, New Jersey, Public Library. Victoria attended Ithaca College, where she majored in Physical Education.

As a boy, Steve Warner was bookish, with a passion for history. One of his earliest interests was the history and culture of the American Indians. Later on, he became fascinated with the history and architecture of the restored colonial capital of Virginia at Williamsburg. He also developed a keen interest in current events, which made him aware of events in South Vietnam long before most of his generation.

Although Steve enjoyed hiking, canoeing, and exploring in various state and national parks, he was neither interested in, nor participated in, any athletic programs. He participated in Cub Scouts, but, curiously, in light of his rather easy adaptation to life in the field in Vietnam, detested the Boy Scouts and quit the program. He also displayed no mechanical ability in his youth.

Steve Warner and his generation were the children of, what I would call, one of the three "hero generations" in American history (the generations that fought the Revolution, The Civil War and World War II). When Steve was born, the fathers of the "baby boomers" had just brought Nazi Germany, Italy's Mussolini and Imperial Japan to their knees. This fact is crucial to understanding why this generation sent its sons to Vietnam. The formative years of the World War II generation, prior to Pearl Harbor, were the years of appeasement of Hitler. After May 1940, the nation engaged in an impassioned and often bitter debate about whether or not America should help save the embattled English from the Nazis, after the astonishing German conquest of France. The lesson learned by the World War II generation was that appeasement only whetted the appetite of dictators. Post-war analysis suggested that a showing of strength against Hitler between 1936 and 1938 might well have prevented World War II. This was a

---

[11] Steve Warner's mother, Esther Warner, and sister, Victoria, provided information about his boyhood and family background to the author on July 17, and August 18, 2002, in written responses to a questionnaire.

major factor in the American decision to draw the line against Communist aggression in Korea, and later in South Vietnam.

With Europe in ruins, the United States emerged from World War II as the most powerful nation on earth. Although the Soviet Union possessed the largest standing army in the world by far, it was a battered, impoverished nation. Its role in the allied victory had been purchased at an infinitely higher price than that of the United States. A backward nation hampered by an obviously inferior economic and political system, the Soviet Union had sustained 6 1/2 million military deaths in the war, compared to several hundred thousand for the United States.[12] Another 20 million Russian civilians had died in the war, compared with virtually none in America. One million of these deaths occurred in Leningrad (now again St Petersburg, a city the size of Chicago) during the 2 1/2 yearlong Nazi siege. Moreover, most of European Russia had been occupied and ravaged by the Germans, while the only American territory to be occupied was the Aleutian Islands.

The Cold War and a Hot War in Korea

Soon however, the so-called Cold War started. The Soviet Army installed Communist governments throughout Eastern Europe. Fear of the Russians and of Communism gripped the United States. Americans became aware of the extraordinary scope of the brutality employed by the Soviet dictator, Joseph Stalin, to preserve and extend his power. Domestic politicians soon began looking for Communist sympathizers in the United States and had no trouble finding individuals in many walks of life who were, or had been, Communist party members or sympathizers. Among left-wing intellectuals in the Democratic Party, there were a number of individuals who flirted with Communism in the 1930s when the Communist movement, particularly in Spain, had been the only organized force actively resisting Fascism and Nazism.

Fear of the Communists at home and abroad increased dramatically when the Soviet Union acquired atomic weapons in 1949. Just as ominous was the spread of what was regarded in the United States as the monolithic Communist movement. Within four years of the end of World War II, the Chinese Communists, under the leadership of Mao Tse-tung, defeated the American supported government of Chiang Kai-shek and established the People's Republic of China to govern the entire Chinese mainland. Americans were aghast at the Communists' widespread executions of real and potential political opponents.

The Communist victory in China came as a particularly devastating blow to the many American missionaries who had been trying to Christianize China since the 19th century. Many of Chiang's supporters concluded that the Democratic administration of President Harry Truman had lost China to the Communists because it was riddled with Communist sympathizers.

---

[12] Slightly less than 300,000 battle deaths; a little over 100,000 other military fatalities.

American fear of Communism intensified in June 1950, when the Army of Communist North Korea invaded non-Communist South Korea. In a quick reversal of policy, the Truman administration decided to send large numbers of American ground forces to South Korea--without bothering to obtain a declaration of war from Congress. Amongst those instrumental in this decision was the Assistant Secretary of State for the Far East, Dean Rusk, a principal architect of the war in Vietnam a decade later, as Secretary of State under Presidents Kennedy and Johnson.

At the outset of the war, the North Koreans easily overran the poorly trained and woefully equipped American and South Korean soldiers. Within weeks, the Americans and their South Korean allies were pushed back to a small area around the southern port of Pusan and were in danger of being pushed off the Korean Peninsula entirely.

The 70 year-old World War I and II hero, General Douglas MacArthur, was given command of the allied troops, now fighting under the auspices of the United Nations. In September 1950, over the strenuous objections of Navy and Marine commanders, MacArthur executed one of the most audacious military maneuvers in history, landing American troops behind the North Koreans at the port of Inchon and quickly rolling up the Communist Army.

General MacArthur, not a shrinking violet to start with, now overplayed his hand. He sent two columns of American soldiers and marines into North Korea in pursuit of the retreating Communists. Ignoring the concerns of subordinates that the two columns were isolated from each other and dismissing warnings about the intervention of the Chinese if he approached their border, MacArthur plunged ahead. In November, his troops were attacked by hundreds of thousands of Chinese Communist soldiers. But for an epic and heroic retreat, followed by evacuation by sea, MacArthur's troops could have been annihilated in the mountains of North Korea.

In this moment of adversity, both MacArthur and President Truman looked to blame the other. Republicans, licking their chops at the prospect of winning back the White House in 1952, after a twenty-year hiatus, made the General's cause their own. When President Truman, with the support of the Joint Chiefs of Staff, relieved General MacArthur from command in 1951 for insubordination, the Republican Party lionized the General at the President's expense.[13] Public opinion overwhelmingly favored General MacArthur rather than the President. Harry Truman's principal alleged shortcoming was his refusal to let General MacArthur win the war, by using nuclear weapons against the Chinese, if need be.

By early 1951, the Korean War was a stalemate. However, many soldiers on both sides died before a truce was arranged between the Communists and America and its

---

[13] The support rendered to General MacArthur by the most prominent Republican in the Senate, Robert A. Taft of Ohio is more than a bit ironic. Senator Taft's father, President William Howard Taft, and MacArthur's father, General Arthur MacArthur, had been bitter enemies at the beginning of the 20th century. The issue between them had been the primacy of civilian authority over the military when Taft was the civilian governor of the Philippines and Arthur MacArthur was the commander of U.S. troops in the islands.

allies. The armistice went into effect six months after Dwight Eisenhower became President in 1953. Essentially, the Communists abandoned their goal of uniting Korea. A major factor in the settlement was the softening of the Communist negotiating positions following the death of the Russian dictator, Joseph Stalin, in March of 1953. In the three years of war, 33,000 Americans died in battle.[14] However, as this war ended, Korea was not the only Asian country threatened by Communism.

The Vietnam War Creeps Up On Stephen Warner And His Generation

When Steve Warner and his generation entered elementary school, many boys played soldier in their father's service caps and read comic books that featured the adventures of American soldiers in Korea. Meanwhile, far removed from the consciousness of most Americans, France, which had ruled Vietnam for 80 years, was about to lose control of the country, as well as the rest of Indochina (Laos and Cambodia) after an eight-year military struggle.

The anti-colonial/nationalist movement in Vietnam was led by a Communist, Ho Chi Minh. In 1954, Ho's Viet Minh overran the French fortress at Dienbienphu and massacred a retreating column in the mountain passes west of An Khe in South Vietnam's central highlands. France decided to call it quits. Consternation reigned in Washington. Members of the Joint Chiefs of Staff and others, including Vice-President Richard Nixon, advocated the use of nuclear weapons to prevent the fall of Vietnam to the Communists. President Eisenhower rejected this advice and decided not to intervene to save Vietnam for France.

However, the United States was not yet ready to concede all of Vietnam to the Communists. At Geneva, Switzerland, in 1954, an international convention agreed to the partition of Vietnam into Communist North Vietnam and a non-Communist South Vietnam. Although the convention agreed the two countries would be united after an election in 1956, the United States immediately began its quest for the establishment of a viable and permanent non-Communist state in the South.

The backbone of this state was two million Catholics who fled the North upon partition, and settled mostly in the area around Saigon. As the leader of this new nation, the United States discovered a bona fide non-Communist Vietnamese nationalist, Ngo Dinh Diem. Unlike most other civilian and military officials in the Saigon government, Diem had not sided with the French during the battle for the end of colonial rule; he had spent most of the time between 1945 and 1955 in exile. However, as it turned out, the Catholic Diem was an autocratic leader who aroused little popular support, particularly amongst the 80% of South Vietnam's inhabitants who were Buddhists. Moreover, support for the Diem regime, which was strongest in the country's cities and towns, was very weak in the rural hamlets in which the vast majority of South Vietnam's peasants lived.

---

[14] There were approximately 20,000 other military fatalities in Korea.

This disaffection of South Vietnam's rural population provided a fertile breeding ground for recruits to the Communist guerilla forces, which were determined to unite South Vietnam with the North. President Eisenhower provided Diem with money and a few hundred American military advisors. The North Vietnamese Government in Hanoi trained, bankrolled and sent officers to lead the guerillas, known as the Viet Cong. The American soldiers who would confront these fighters referred to them by their initials, "VC" or "Charlie" or, with begrudging admiration as "Sir Charles." Beginning in 1960, the Viet Cong became increasingly more aggressive in their attacks on the government.

When Steve Warner was in ninth grade, John F. Kennedy was elected President of the United States by the narrowest of margins. Steve's father, Harold, voted for Richard Nixon. In his inaugural address of January 20, 1961, the President promised that Americans would "pay any price, bear any burden…to assure the survival and the success of liberty." Over the next twelve years, a generation of Americans would learn just what that phrase could mean when carried to its extreme.

As Kennedy took office, the nation was preoccupied with the struggle for supremacy with what was regarded as the Communist bloc, led by the Soviet Union and in concert, it was assumed, by Communist China. The nation was still reeling from the establishment by Fidel Castro in Cuba, of the first Communist government in the western hemisphere. The first major action taken by Kennedy with regard to the worldwide conflict with Communism was the support of an attack by anti-Castro refugees on Cuba at the Bay of Pigs in April 1961. The administration inherited the plan for this assault from the Eisenhower administration; however, Kennedy bore responsibility for the complete disaster that transpired when Castro repulsed the invasion, killing and capturing hundreds of anti-Communist Cuban soldiers.

President Kennedy, although genuinely concerned with Communist expansion, was equally concerned with the potential that more Communist victories would provide to his Republican detractors. He knew that if Vietnam fell to the Communists, the Republicans would accuse him of losing it, as they blamed Truman for losing China and not winning the war in Korea. Given his slim margin of victory in 1960, Kennedy could not afford to give the Republicans additional ammunition with which to campaign if he hoped to be re-elected in 1964.

Our response to the 1950 invasion of South Korea is fundamental to understanding our response to the prospect of a Communist victory in South Vietnam a decade later--a theme to which I will return. One major difference between the two wars is the degree of support the United States received from other nations in the free world. Britain, France, Canada and Turkey were among the nations contributing to defense of South Korea. None of our European allies provided troops to assist our efforts to save South Vietnam.[15] In fact, in contrast to Korea, most of our allies were indifferent or opposed to American military involvement in Vietnam.

---

[15] The western allies and the Germans themselves were hesitant to encourage any military activity on the part of West Germany. This was due to the danger of exacerbating tensions with the Soviets and Communist East Germany and the lingering fear of German militarism.

Important Asian nations that we were supposedly protecting from Communism by fighting in Vietnam were also totally unconcerned with the outcome of the War. The Washington Post on October 7, 1965 reported a speech by the United States Ambassador to Tokyo, Edwin Reischauer, in which he urged the Japanese to drop their "apathetic attitude towards the Vietnam conflict."[16]Despite all the blood and treasure we invested in Vietnam, neither Japan nor India ever awakened to the dire threat supposedly facing them in the event of a Communist takeover in South Vietnam.

Indeed, with the exception of South Korea itself, the nations supposedly immediately threatened by a Communist victory in South Vietnam, provided relatively small numbers of troops (Australia, New Zealand, Thailand and the Philippines) or none (Burma, Indonesia, Japan and India). Moreover, the United States paid all the expenses for the commitment of South Korean, Thai and Filipino soldiers and provided South Korean businessmen many opportunities to profit from the War.

Throughout his short tenure as president, Kennedy markedly increased the number of American military advisors in South Vietnam from 700 to 15,000. The number of American casualties began increasing as well.[17]

Steve Warner's senior year at Princeton High School in New Jersey began in September 1963. That year he shared his room with a foreign exchange student from Sweden. An excellent student, with high SAT scores, Steve had his heart set on attending Brown University in Providence, Rhode Island. Much to his dismay, he was not accepted by Brown, probably due to his lack of extra curricular activities. Steve ended up settling for his "safety school," Gettysburg College, a small liberal arts school in the town that was the site of the most famous Civil War battle. Gettysburg, Pennsylvania, was also the retirement home of former President Dwight D. Eisenhower until his death in 1969.

Nineteen sixty-three turned out to be a watershed year in the Vietnam conflict. The United States gave up on Ngo Dinh Diem, the man we had chosen to lead South Vietnam in 1956. Diem had antagonized many of the country's Buddhists. Having already survived an attempted coup d'etat and the bombing of the presidential palace, Diem was more concerned with staffing his country's army with commanders he could rely on than with officers who were competent and willing to fight the Communist Viet Cong .

On November 1, 1963, South Vietnamese Army (ARVN) officers overthrew Diem with the acquiescence of the United States Government, and then murdered him. Three weeks later President Kennedy was assassinated in Dallas, Texas. While Kennedy's death was followed by a relatively smooth transition of power to his Vice-

---

[16] *The Washington Post,* October 7, 1965, A4, Col. 3.

[17] While there has been much speculation as to what would have happened in Vietnam had President Kennedy lived beyond 1963, it is just as interesting to speculate what would have happened had Eisenhower not been barred from seeking a third term. Eisenhower had resisted the temptation to intervene in Vietnam in 1954. Given his status as a military hero, it is indeed possible that Eisenhower as President would have avoided the disastrous policies of his successors.

President, Lyndon B. Johnson (LBJ), political instability followed the death of President Diem. President Johnson and his advisors feared that Diem's successors might take the advice of French President Charles DeGaulle and enter into a coalition with the Communists. Many thousands of Vietnamese and Americans would not have died over the course of the next ten years had we allowed them to do so. Moreover, the retribution that followed the Communist victory may well have been less severe. General Nguyen Khanh, who emerged as the country's leader in 1964 was trusted by no one.

Johnson, running for President in his own right in 1964, became very concerned that South Vietnam would fall to the Communists during his presidency and feared that such an eventuality would doom his chances for enacting very ambitious domestic reforms in the United States. Chief among those was a "war against poverty" and an end to racial segregation. The latter, in addition to being a moral issue, threatened to undermine America's ability to combat Communism in the underdeveloped nations of Africa and Asia. In the 1964 election, Steve Warner's father, Harold, voted for the Republican candidate, Barry Goldwater.

Lyndon Johnson and his advisors determined in 1964 that, without a large infusion of American troops, South Vietnam would fall to the Communists. First the President seized upon an alleged North Vietnamese attack on two American destroyers in August 1964 to obtain from Congress authority to engage the U.S. military in Vietnam as he saw fit. Now it is known that not only did these attacks not occur but that the U.S. Navy was inviting attack by supporting South Vietnamese commando attacks on North Vietnam.

The result, the Gulf of Tonkin Resolution, was passed unanimously in the House of Representatives. Two Democrats had to audacity to vote against it in the Senate--in the face of opinion polls showing that 85 percent of the American public was behind President Johnson. These two were Senator Wayne Morse of Oregon--generally regarded a "loose cannon," and Ernest Gruening of Alaska. Morse predicted that supporters of the resolution "would live to regret it." His prediction certainly proved true for a number of the Senate Democrats, notably two who would become the most prominent critics of the war, the head of the foreign relations committee, J. William Fulbright of Arkansas, and George McGovern of South Dakota. Gruening warned that "all of Vietnam is not worth the life of a single American boy."[18]

President Johnson was already planning to commit large numbers of U.S. ground forces to South Vietnam. He and his military advisors determined that by inflicting heavy losses on Communist forces, the United States would force North Vietnam and the Viet Cong, to acquiesce in the survival of a non-Communist South Vietnamese Government. Few greater miscalculations have ever been made in American History.

---

[18] Gruening came to the Tonkin debate with impeccable "dovish" credentials. He had been the publicity chairman for Senator Robert M. LaFollette's presidential campaign in 1924. LaFollette, who had stood virtually alone against the clamor for U.S. participation in World War I, would have been very proud of his protégé in August 1964.

In February 1965, Johnson seized upon a Communist attack on the U.S. Air Force base at Pleiku as the opportunity to begin sending American ground combat troops to Vietnam. Initially, the Administration said that these troops were being sent only to protect American air and naval installations. However, Johnson and his on-site military commander, General William C. Westmoreland, had planned from the outset to send American troops into the Vietnamese countryside to search for and destroy the Communist forces.

The Vietnam War was overwhelmingly popular for the first three years that American troops were fighting the Communists. The Republican Party was even more hawkish than the administration. Richard Nixon, for one, made sure that President Johnson appreciated the potential political consequences of a Communist victory in Vietnam. Nixon, embarking upon his miraculous comeback after losing the presidency in 1960 and the gubernatorial race in California in 1962, visited Saigon for three days in early September 1965. Upon his departure, Nixon held a news conference in which he announced that he opposed any negotiations with the Communists unless the North Vietnamese were willing to withdraw their forces from the South. *New York Times* correspondent Neil Sheehan reported that:

> Mr. Nixon warned that if President Johnson compromised with the Communists, the Republican Party would make Vietnam a campaign issue next year in the Congressional election and in 1968 during the Presidential campaign.

Nixon predicted that:

> [The War] is likely to go on militarily for two or three or four more years. We should be ready to participate for that long. We cannot afford to leave without a victory over aggression.

The former Vice-President also suggested that the commitment of 125,000 U.S. troops, recently announced by LBJ, would prove to be too little. He opined that, "our commitment will have to be more substantial and larger than we have at present."[19]

Opposition to the war was limited to what was generally regarded as fringe elements on a few very liberal university campuses--primarily on the East and West Coasts. Most college students thought very little about the war and at least passively supported it, largely because, due to the student deferments, it didn't affect them directly.

In its early years, the Vietnam War was also a very marketable item of popular culture. One of the best selling books in 1965 was Robin Moore's novel, *The Green Berets,* which for many college males was the only unassigned book they read during their undergraduate careers. Two years later, Sergeant Barry Sadler's, *The Ballad of the Green Berets,* was the number one single record in the United States for five consecutive weeks. Over eleven million copies of the stirring melody were sold.

---

[19] *The New York Times,* September 6, 1965, 1:6.

Gettysburg College, with a total enrollment of about 1,800 students, was not atypical. Prior to the Communists' Tet offensive of 1968, only a handful of its students actively opposed American military involvement in Vietnam. Steve Warner, however, began to become very troubled by the war during his freshman year at Gettysburg, 1964-65, and by his junior year was openly expressing his opposition to it. In October 1967, during his senior year, Steve and a few others from Gettysburg went to Washington, D.C. to participate in a huge anti-war march on the Pentagon. Also during that year, Steve and a few friends, including John Schiller, visited a fraternity house on campus, to proselytize the members about the war. They were not well received.

At the beginning, the war was being fought largely by professional soldiers and young men who had voluntarily chosen to serve in Army or Marines. The latter were generally economically disadvantaged youth from rural areas and the inner cities. Due to the fact that college students were entitled to a deferment from conscription, few dreamed in 1964 and 1965 that the war would last long enough that it would ever impact them. However, some students who dropped out or flunked out of school, or simply carried too few credits, soon found themselves in the jungles of South Vietnam. The war was very tough on those young men who were late bloomers. One of these was PFC Lynn Ferguson of Russells Point, Ohio. After dropping out of Miami University, Ferguson was drafted and sent to Vietnam as a medic. On March 6, 1967, after little over three weeks in Vietnam, he was killed trying to aid a wounded infantryman. His mother was so angered by her son's fate that she insisted that Lynn's body be taken out of his Army uniform and dressed in civilian clothes before burial.[20]

The press, almost without exception, supported the Vietnam War at the outset. Parallels were drawn between the situation in Vietnam and that which had faced the European democracies 1938. In November of that year, at a meeting in Munich, the English Prime Minister Neville Chamberlain and the French Prime Minister Edward Daladier had given in to Adolph Hitler's demands for a chunk of Czechoslovakia. This apparently whetted Hitler's appetite and convinced him that he need not worry about a military response to his further aggression.

In 1964 and 1965, the administration's argument, that a show of strength was needed to show the Communists that America had the backbone to stop aggression, was widely accepted. At *The Washington Post*, later a major critic of American policy in Vietnam, this view was repeatedly endorsed on the editorial page. Chalmers Roberts, in his history of the newspaper, recalled:

James Russell Wiggins [the Post's managing editor until 1968] was not a mindless hawk; he was repelled by all-out war proponents. Essentially, like many of his generation within the administration, Wiggins was influenced by memory of the democracies' failure to check the aggression that had led to World War II. This

---

[20] My source regarding this incident is the second hand account of my college roommate, James R. Myers, from nearby Lakeview, Ohio, whose sister attended the funeral.

was a central theme of Post editorials on Vietnam and no amount of argument that Vietnam bore no resemblance to Europe cold shake Wiggins from his principle.[21]

The New York Times was more in the mode of fence straddling at the outset of the war--by repeatedly advocating [or wishing for] a negotiated settlement. On June 11, 1965, *The Times* reported that the administration had alerted parts of three Army divisions for movement to Vietnam, and that Major General Nguyen Van Thieu was attempting to form yet another new government in Saigon. *The Times* did not respond to these developments with an editorial. However, C. L. Sulzberger, a columnist related to the owners of the paper, bought the domino theory, hook, line and sinker.

> One fundamental point remains. The United States must somehow manage to hold firm in Vietnam. A collapse there would endanger not only Southeast and South Asia but also those other regions on which China has its eye--Africa and Latin America.[22]

On the same page, James Reston, *The Times'* star columnist, expressed a somewhat different take on developments in Saigon. After reporting that the effectiveness of the South Vietnamese Army was "far more disappointing" than any official would admit, Reston stated that "responsible officials" at the Pentagon were not sure the war could be won with 300,000 American troops. Thus, the administration was left with a choice of 1) leaving it up to the South Vietnamese to win the war with our assistance and advice; or 2) muddling through by increasing the number of U.S. troops in the hope that the South Vietnamese could be encouraged sufficiently to prevail. The first course, Reston noted was "tantamount to accepting defeat."

In its search for good copy, the national press also gave a great deal of publicity to the most extreme and outrageous personalities in the anti-war movement, such as the exhibitionists Abbie Hoffman and Jerry Rubin. Their antics provided much more interesting fare than sober reflection about where we were headed in Vietnam. Much attention was also given to reports of harassing telephone calls received by the families of soldiers serving in Vietnam, ostensibly made by opponents of the war. Unfortunately, the public's general hostility to such radical personalities made it even more unfashionable to oppose the growing American military commitment than it otherwise would have been.

College Newspaper Columnist

At Gettysburg College, Steve Warner participated in more extra-curricular activities than he had in high school. He joined the staff of the college newspaper, *The Gettysburgian*, for which he became a regular columnist and then features editor. In his sophomore year, he wrote a column in the October 8, 1965 edition, responding to another student's harangue against "the peace mongers." This individual expressed a widely held view of anti-war demonstrators.

---

[21] Roberts, Chalmers, *The Washington Post*, 1977, at pp 373-4.
[22] *The New York Times*, June 11, 1965, 30:3.

What they [our soldiers in Vietnam] do mind, however, is fighting and dying for their nation and then picking up a hometown newspaper and reading of a peace march or teach-in. The visage of a lot of hypocritical leftist professors, draft-dodging youth and other ill-assorted traitors debunking our efforts in this way only serves to demoralize these men.[23]

Steve responded, arguing that, "a society like ours cannot live without such troublemakers and cause-seekers."

The 'good people' are too enmeshed in their own little world to care about civil rights in Selma or villages burned without reason in Vietnam. Only once in a while after the cause-seekers and trouble-makers have brought such situations to his attention does the good citizen show a little interest and initiative.

Steve organized a human relations forum at the college, which focused on social justice in the local community. On November 11, 1966, he was one of eight students to sign a letter in *The Gettysburgian* announcing the founding of an "ad hoc committee of students who are opposed to the war in Vietnam." A month earlier, on October 7, 1966 the paper published his article entitled, "Let's Stop Fighting Communism," a first attempt by Steve to come to terms with the Vietnam War.

It is time the United States stopped fighting communism. It is also time that supposedly intelligent and patriotic Americans stopped their childish denouncements of communism and their equally childish lauding of democracy and capitalism. They are simply words which a world gone mad with "ism" has distorted to the point of the ridiculous.

Neither communism, democracy nor capitalism is worth shedding blood over, for each is meaningless or more exactly so full of meanings that it no longer denotes a single identifiable concept...

The great tragedy and danger of the Vietnam War is that the vast majority of Americans refuse to see it in terms other than the meaningless generalizations of stopping Communist aggression, preserving democracy and protecting South Vietnam's sovereignty. Such patterns may be soothing in justifying the sending of "our boys" to Vietnam, but as refuges from the realities of the situation, they lead to disaster. They strengthen the trend toward making the war into a black and white issue and raising it to the level of a crusade. Even worse, they permit the United States to fight a war without forcing her to define what the war is being fought for in specific terms. The whole concept of a negotiated settlement, a compromise, is threatened, for until the majority of American citizens know specifically what they are fighting for, the American Government cannot sit down at the negotiation table and hammer out a compromise acceptable to public opinion. The only alternatives to a compromise are U.S. withdrawal or continued

---

[23] *The Gettysburgian*, October 1, 1965, 1.

escalation. The former is unlikely and the later terrifying, as it acknowledges no power in the war but brute force.

The great barrier to peace in Vietnam is not the small group of true doves, hawks and undecides. These individuals recognize the war for the complex situation it is, even if they do not agree what should be done. They can press for peace because they have established in their own minds what America is fighting for, be it the unconditional surrender of North Vietnam or simply keeping the Communists from gaining anything beyond a united Communist Vietnam.

The great barrier to peace is the huge majority of Americans, Gettysburg students and faculty included, which might, for a lack of a better name, be called pseudo-doves, hawks and undecides. These people consider the Vietnam conflict a trite subject to talk and write about and justify their beliefs concerning the war with meaningless statements about fighting communism.

This coming week the Chapel Council is sponsoring two lectures…The subject matter can only be trite to those who see Vietnam in the meaningless terms of fighting communism--the people who would have America fight her way into World War III.

This article shows that at least Steve was thinking about Vietnam, at a time when most college students, except those in danger of flunking out of school and being drafted were not thinking about it all. Given the availability of student deferments through graduate school, all one had to do to avoid Vietnam was stay in school until age 26. To most students in 1966, the war was a peripheral concern, one, which had no realistic chance of affecting them personally.

However, it is hard to determine the point of the article or agree with any of its premises--apart from its condemnation of apathy. The U.S. government never sought the "unconditional surrender" of North Vietnam in the sense that it sought the unconditional surrender of Germany and Japan in World War II. President Johnson, and later President Nixon, realized that to invade North Vietnam would risk war with Communist China and bring the world to brink of World War III. Thus, they relied on what now appear to have been half-measures to preserve the Saigon government.

The premise behind the American war effort was that by applying overwhelming force we could convince North Vietnam to agree to tolerate the existence of an independent, non-communist South Vietnam. We had accomplished something quite similar in Korea a decade before. As it turned out, containing communism in Vietnam was much more difficult than doing so in Korea. First of all, the fact that South Korea is a peninsula made stopping infiltration from the North much easier than stopping infiltration into South Vietnam, through the jungles and mountains of Laos and Cambodia. Secondly, we vastly underestimated the willingness of the Vietnamese communists to take casualties and the degree of support, active and passive, that they enjoyed in the countryside of South Vietnam.

Moreover, as ridiculous as it seems now, the Johnson Administration, with Republicans such as Richard Nixon, applying considerable political pressure, was telling the American people that the existence of a non-communist South Vietnam was essential to the security of the rest of southeast Asia, which in turn was essential to the security of the United States. A Communist victory in South Vietnam, we were told, would endanger other countries in the region; Thailand, Burma and even India, Japan and Australia. This contention was predicated in part on the proposition that North Vietnam was a stalking horse for Communist China. In retrospect, it is hard to understand how anyone could believe that whether India, Australia and Japan went communist depended to any degree on whether the Saigon government survived. Harder yet to understand is the proposition that a Communist victory in South Vietnam endangered the government and people of the United States.

Conversely, proponents of the war never explained how "standing firm" in Vietnam would lead any other country, such as Thailand, to conclude that the United States would send another half million GIs to help combat a Communist insurgency. Indeed, sending so many of our young men to Vietnam made it less likely that any other country would receive any significant American assistance in the form of manpower.

As the war dragged on, the few opponents of the war became more active on the Gettysburg campus and Steve Warner's views of the war became more focused. On February 10, 1967, he wrote a column entitled "What Would You Do?" opposing the American bombing of North Vietnam. He asked rhetorically, "why should our selective bombing of strategic points in North Vietnam lead that nation to give up?" To the contrary, Steve opined, the bombing would likely only strengthen the Communists' resolve. Steve argued further that:

> The essence of this proposal is that the bombing be ended in such a manner as to let Hanoi portray it as a major victory. Only with such a face saving accomplishment behind her can she hope to de-escalate without upsetting her own internal and external political balance. The present Hanoi ruling group does not wish to be tagged defeatist any more than the reigning group in a Western nation would so desire under similar circumstances.

In his column, Steve assumes that the North Vietnamese were looking for a face-saving way out the War. That was never the case. The Communists never wavered from their goal to unite Vietnam and time and time again demonstrated that there was no limit to the resources and lives they were willing to spend to achieve this goal.

Steve traveled to Arlington, Virginia, with some friends to participate in an anti-war march on the Pentagon in October 1967. When he returned, Steve wrote an excellent article for *The Gettysburgian* entitled "Middle Class Carnival."[24]

---

[24] October 27, 1967 edition.

(The following article was written Saturday night before I heard or read any extensive news coverage of the march. Though the news media played up the violence this is not the view I gained as a participant.

Remember that the mob of 3,000 who, according to the Sunday *New York Times*, breached the security lines surrounding the Pentagon at 5:40 p.m. was only about 6% of the total number of marchers and that the "at least 51 people" arrested on Saturday... represented slightly over one arrest for every 1,000 marchers.)

The Peace March went off as scheduled Saturday. Only one thing, the whole affair smacked more of a carnival than a crusade.

Since the march to the Pentagon did not actually get under way until about 2:30 p.m. and the rally at the Lincoln Memorial began at 11:30 a.m., there were three hours to mill around, and that is exactly what thousands did. Some sought friends from other schools. At times, the whole affair reminded one of nothing more than a college homecoming. Most people, however, just gaped. Here was a collection of sideshows which would humble P. T. Barnum.

General X was prancing around on our left. With three little plastic military planes taped to his hat and a chest full of colored ribbons, this pathetic soul begged for your attention. And what was this pseudo-general's message? "Smoke grass, not bananas. Forget about the war and live. Everyone is getting high on POTatoes."

A few yards further on, all prim and proper, sat the Women's League for Peace, a group which reminded one of nothing more than a church social. These neatly clothed matrons clustered on the grass, munched their tot 'em lunches, and radiated a feeling of quiet, motherly determination.

But let's continue on through this carnival of clashing characters. As the helicopters whirled overhead, the speeches at the foot of the Lincoln Memorial faded into a blur. "Was that Dick Gregory or Doctor Spock? Did you hear Joan Baez, or was it Jefferson Airplane? Who knows and further, who really cares? What is that crowd up ahead?"

Passing signs proclaimed "Beat LBJ into a plowshare," "Che Lives," and "Lady Bird Smokes," one was suddenly confronted by a hairy chested young fellow jumping up and down and proclaiming: "Hell I'm not here because of the War. I don't really give a damn about it. I've got a life to live. Smoke pot."

The crowd moved on. "This is a big farce here," remarks someone. "Kill the War," retorts a poster.

Who were these fifty thousand milling individuals gathered on a beautiful October Saturday to march for peace? According to the "Fact Sheet" more than

24

fifteen different groupings were expected. Yet whatever banner they chose to march under, this whole seething mass, was beneath the variety of its costumes, middle class America.

The number of Negroes was minimal. This was a march of white middle class America. Hippies were there, but if you looked more closely, these individuals' beautiful costumes often showed more devotion to being the center of attraction than to renunciation of the material world. And for every hippie there were two immaculately dressed mods, and for every mod a scrufty; and for every scrufty, two or three neat "ideal type" middle class folk, whether college students with tweed sports jackets and elegant sweaters, or middle-aged suit clad veterans.

Perhaps the spirit of the crowd was best shown when the march actually began. According to the press and the speakers at the foot of Lincoln, this was to be a direct action undertaking. "Confront the war makers," the posters screamed. "We shall physically block the halls and doors of the Pentagon." "Hell No, We Won't Go."

The march did not start at 1:30 as scheduled but at 2:30 for some and not [un]till 4:00 or 4:30 for the last. Was there violence in the ranks? Discontentment? Fury? Why, no. Everyone sat down on the grass and visited. What did they talk about? Vietnam? A little. Mostly they remarked that there was no place to get lunch and couldn't someone make a fortune selling hot dogs or soft drinks. It was assumed that you opposed the war so why talk about it?

Patience and docility were the keynote of the day. When the marshals, the march's own informal police force told the marchers to link arms and walk fifteen abreast, 50,000 people linked arms and marched fifteen abreast. When the marshals told the marchers to stop for no apparent reason, the marchers stopped. When a marshal came walking through the grass beside the Pentagon parking lot and announced that the marchers were subject to arrest for sprawling on the grass, numerous individuals, though by no means all, docilely moved off the grass and sat down in the prescribed parking lot. This was middle-class America with respect for law and order so ingrained into it that even when it gathered 50,000 strong to protest a war, it still obeyed the rules.

Why did this, the great "1967 Direct Action Peace March," become the "1967 Middle-Class - Obey - The Rules Peace March?" For one thing, it cost a lot to attend. Most people seemed to be from out of town. Thousands came from New York and thousands more from New England. They came by bus and train. Many stayed overnight. Even going down from Gettysburg by scheduled bus cost close to ten dollars when one compensated at dinner for the lunch he never ate. Who could afford to go but middle-class America?

Most, no doubt, would assume that the march was a failure from the above descriptions, and yet I think they would be wrong. Few in the crowd seemed to feel the march would have any direct effect on Washington's policy. What it did do was to give 50,000 people, who do want the war to end, an emotional and spiritual bond among themselves, from which to draw and strengthen hopes and beliefs during the coming months. In this sense, the march was closely akin to those great political carnivals called national party conventions. Neither the mass convention nor the mass march is an efficient medium through which to get things done. They do, however, strengthen the spirit and determination of the sincere participant.

Fifty thousand people may not sound like many, but they are enough to make a line fifteen men abreast from the Lincoln Memorial to the Pentagon more than twice over. To be able to draw from the feeling that comes from being part of such a group can help one move mountains. It can help to overcome the heartbreak and frustration of the coming months as individuals do their little bit to stop the war and see their efforts go apparently for naught. If Pat can keep up the effort at Radcliffe and if John is willing to go to jail rather than fight, and if 50,000 other middle class people of all varieties are willing to march for peace, then the least you can do, wherever you may be, is to continue your little effort to convince middle-class America that the war is wrong.

Cynics on both the right and left will laugh that these are fools, for the masses, even if convinced the war is wrong, cannot force a change in policy. But these cynics are wrong, and if they are not wrong they are hypocrites and fools for mouthing love of America and pledging allegiance to the democratic Republic.

In the month after this demonstration, November 1967, the anti-war Senator Eugene McCarthy, from Minnesota, announced that he would run against President Johnson for the Democratic Presidential nomination in 1968. The same month, General Westmoreland returned to the United States and left most of the American public with the impression that the war was being won and was winding down.

For example, before the National Press Club on November 21, 1967, the General stated:

I am absolutely certain that whereas in 1965 the enemy was winning, today he is certainly losing.

***

It is significant that the enemy has not won a major battle in more than a year. In general, he can fight his large forces only at the edges of his sanctuaries.

Soon to be proved wrong on the last point, Westmoreland went on to state that the Viet Cong had to increasingly depend on replacements from North Vietnam. He did not offer an opinion as to whether the Communists would be able to continue to fight the war with regular North Vietnamese troops. Nor did he estimate how long and how many American lives it would take to ensure the survival of South Vietnam if the Communists were able to fight in South Vietnam with North Vietnamese replacements.

The General described four phases of the American-South Vietnamese battle plan. The third phase he stated would begin in 1968. He did not predict how long this third phase would last. During the fourth phase, the ARVN would be responsible for "mopping up" the Viet Cong. In this phase, the American forces, he promised, would become increasingly superfluous.[25] McCarthy's campaign was going nowhere--but in a few months this would change.

Tet 1968 And The End Of Graduate Student Deferments

The spring of 1968 was a turning point for many Americans with regard to the Vietnam War. The Communist Tet offensive, which started on January 31, 1968, demonstrated, if nothing else, that an American victory was not imminent, and that a large commitment of American troops would have to stay in South Vietnam and suffer significant causalities indefinitely to preserve the non-Communist government in Saigon. The Communists attacked virtually every major city and town in the country. While suffering ferocious casualties themselves, the VC and NVA inflicted unprecedented casualties on American and ARVN forces.

The number of GIs killed in Vietnam each week jumped from 203 in the week of January 27, to February 3, 1968 to over 500 per week from February 11, through March 2.[26] The Communists forces captured a fortress in Hue, the second largest city in South Vietnam, and held it for several weeks until driven out by the ARVN and U.S. Marines. During their occupation of parts of the city, it is estimated that the Communists executed 3,000 civilians. The VC also staged a spectacular attack in Saigon, in which a commando squad got inside the United States Embassy compound, where they fought a pitched battle until wiped out. The ferocity of the fighting was also reflected by the Nazi-style murder of over two hundred unarmed Vietnamese civilians at the village of Mylai in March 1968 by an American infantry company, one platoon of which was under the command of Lt. William Calley.

Immediately upon the heels of Tet, the Johnson administration announced a fundamental change in the way the selective service system operated. As the war dragged on, and American casualties mounted, the administration became very sensitive to the fact that the war was being fought primarily by young men from the lower echelons of society. There was a growing sense that it was unfair that one could stay in school until the age of 26 and avoid the draft. In February 1968, the administration announced that, with the exception of medical and veterinary students, deferments for graduate students would be abolished.[27]

---

[25] *The New York Times,* November 22, 1967, p. 2.

[26] The worst week of the war in terms of GIs killed actually occurred two months later. During the week of May 5 - 11, 1968, 616 American soldiers were killed in Vietnam, Ronald Spector, *After Tet,* Appendix 2.

[27] Undergraduate deferments continued throughout the Vietnam War. President Nixon was authorized to end undergraduate deferments in September 1971 but did so in a manner to exempt the entire college class of 1975. In December 1971, Secretary of Defense Melvin Laird announced there would be no draft calls in early 1972 and announced an end to the draft in January 1973.

Upon graduation, most students would thus be reclassified into category 1-A, i.e., immediately subject to induction. Thousands of college students, who were about to graduate, became vulnerable to the draft for the first time. Because they had so little time to adjust to this situation, those men most effected by the change were those of the college class of 1968, which included Steve Warner at Gettysburg College, William Jefferson Clinton at Georgetown and George W. Bush at Yale.

Members of the class of 1969, which included Albert Gore, Jr., at Harvard and Dan Quayle at DePauw, at least had an extra year to find a way to avoid Vietnam service.[28] Many members of the college class of 1970 were to be beneficiaries of a newly implemented draft lottery. The first lottery drawing occurred on December 1, 1969, after Steve Warner had been in the Army for six months. His birthdate, February 21, was the 363rd number drawn. Anyone in the lottery with a number that high would never have been drafted under any circumstances.

With the change of the draft rules, many young men who had paid scant attention to the War began to scrutinize its justification much more closely. While the anti-war movement had a substantial number of adherents prior to 1968, it numbers swelled dramatically all over the country as a lot of people untouched by the war previously were now faced with the possibility that it might affect them or their friends and loved ones directly. This was made evident in dramatic increase in Senator McCarthy's support among Democratic voters in New Hampshire. In mid-February 1968, polls indicated that he would receive less than 20 percent of the vote in the primary. However, the primary was held at the end of February when the implications of the Tet offensive began to sink in. President Johnson received only 300 more votes than McCarthy out of 50,000 cast.

At Gettysburg College, an increasing number of students and faculty members, who had either ignored the war previously or passively assented to government policy, changed their tune. One hundred eighty four individuals signed an anti-war petition in February 1968. This was viewed as a great advance by one of the supporters when compared to "the minimal participation" in a "Peace Week" sponsored by anti-war students in 1967. The last paragraph of the petition proclaimed:

> We believe, therefore, that our government must reverse its course and move toward the only sane solution: de-escalation, recognition of the need to include the National Liberation Front [Viet Cong] in any future South Vietnamese government and eventual withdrawal of American troops.[29]

---

[28] Gore served two years in the Army as an enlisted man. He spent five months, January 2, 1971 - May 1971, in Vietnam as an Army journalist at Bien Hoa. Had there been space for him, he would have ended up at the USARV PIO with Steve Warner. According to a *Washington Post* profile of December 31, 1999, one of Steve's co-workers, a friend of Gore's from Ft. Rucker, Alabama, took Gore to the PIO upon his arrival in Vietnam to see whether he could be assigned there. Bush and Quayle joined National Guard units.

[29] *The Gettysburgian,* February 16, 1968.

However, Steve Warner criticized the timing of the petition. In an article in the February 16, 1968 *Gettysburgian* entitled "Why Now?" his arguments at times bore similarities to the those who generally castigated the opponents of the war.

This week's petition against the Vietnam War may be the right type of petition but it is offered very definitely at the wrong time.

The petition must be considered a response triggered by the current Viet Cong and North Vietnamese offensive. Otherwise there is no way to explain this particular moment for ending the four months of near silence among the campus war critics.

***

Hanoi could only interpret our de-escalation in the midst of their biggest offensive as a sign of weakness and thus a reason to press on harder. Why should the National Liberation Front accept mere inclusion in a South Vietnamese government when, with a bit more of a push, U.S.-South Vietnamese de-escalation might be turned into panic? This could result in the N. L. F. acquiring the whole government of South Vietnam.

President Johnson states that the present offensive is the Viet Cong's last and that, if the Viet Cong are halted this time, they are through...

If this current offensive is the enemy's last and the United States and South Vietnam do block it, then the military aspect of the war--aside from minor guerilla activity--will have ended without the need of the United States casting doubt on the value of her mutual defense treaties. The major job of peaceful reconstruction of South Vietnam can then begin, even if no formal understanding can be reached with Hanoi.

If this current offensive is the enemy's last and the United States and South Vietnam fail to stop it, there will finally exist a dramatic concrete and visible manifestation of the United States' military failure in Vietnam. The opportunity will then exist to enlist many new Americans--possibly an electoral majority--in demanding a U.S. withdrawal from Vietnam.

If this current offensive is not the enemy's last, this fact should also become obvious fairly soon after the offensive ends. Hanoi will do her best before August and November to force President Johnson to call in more troops beyond the current 525,000 men, and thus force Johnson to admit that Hanoi's strength is not yet broken, and that the U.S. is in for a very long, very bloody war if she wants to keep South Vietnam noncommunist.

***

If the Vietnam situation should develop even partially into this situation of failure, the moment would have come, at least for me, when the United States' twin goals of a non-communist South Vietnam and the preservation of the myth of U.S. military invincibility would cease to be worth the cost. We should then de-escalate, seek to get the N.L.F. into the South Vietnamese Government and rapidly prepare the way for a peaceful communist takeover in South Vietnam.

It is then that the petitions will be needed, along with the votes, to give Washington the mandate and the backing it will need in order to admit that our Vietnam policy has failed and should therefore be radically changed.

At the time of this article, then, Steve's position appears to have shifted. He seems to be saying that if victory has almost been won, then preservation of a non-communist South Vietnam is a desirable goal if it can be attained at a reasonable cost. In a letter published the following week, he emphasized that while he agreed with the signers of the petition generally, he took issue with their recommendation for an American response during the Communist Tet offensive. Steve stated:

My objections to the February 16 petition were not to the points made in regard to protesting the war. The War in Vietnam contains much worth protesting at any time...

I can not see how a program [recommending de-escalation and recognition of the NLF] has any immediate relevance, practical application, in the midst of a major offensive initiated by the enemy in a truce period. The program had validity before the offensive began and it may well have validity when the offensive is over but the program does not have validity during the offensive.

Both the petition and Steve's commentary on it drew criticism from other students. Signers of the petition, familiar with Steve's long-standing opposition to the conduct of the war, expressed bewilderment at his critique. Another student reiterated the dangers of appeasing the Viet Cong and expressed continued confidence "in the integrity and patriotism" of the administration in Washington. Still another observed that the less than 200 signatures on the petition was "hardly an impressive showing" given a college community of 2,000 people.[30]

Farewell to Gettysburg

By the spring of his senior year, Steve was actively considering dropping out of Gettysburg College to work full time on McCarthy's campaign. His father convinced him to stay in school. He did, however, spend some time campaigning for Senator McCarthy. Had Steve dropped out to work in the campaign he would have lost his student deferment and been subject to immediate induction into the Armed Forces.

---

[30] *The Gettysburgian,* February 23, 1968.

During the spring of 1968, the Vietnam War cast an ever-increasing shadow over the Gettysburg campus. Forty students protested a visit by recruiters from Dow Chemical Company, the manufacturers of Napalm, a chemical used in Vietnam to burn away vegetation but also used against enemy troops--and sometimes, accidentally, on Vietnamese civilians.

On March 1, 1968, the Army ROTC unit at the college announced the branch assignments for graduating seniors. Only two were assigned to the infantry, but fifteen cadets received artillery branch assignments and seven were going to be armor officers [i.e., tanks]. Among the noncombat branch assignments were six for the quartermaster corps [supply]; three to the corps of engineers, six to the military police, five to the signal corps, two to the adjutant general's corps and four to intelligence and security.[31] On March 8, Steve authored a purely factual piece, entitled "Draft Tightens Noose on Future Scholars."

By the time of his graduation from Gettysburg in June 1968, Steve stood 5' 11" and had a rather slender build. He had blue eyes, wore glasses and had straight thick light brown hair. Even his friends describe him as "nerdy" or having the presence of an absent-minded professor. They recall him often walking around with part of his shirttails hanging out.

His friend, John Schiller, recalls Steve as the fastest reader he ever met and describes him as a "human vacuum" of information.[32] According to Schiller, Steve was a person who had many acquaintances, but few close friends. Schiller, is convinced, not simply on Steve's paper credentials, that had he lived, Steve Warner would have "made a difference" to society. Moreover, he believes that Steve was more than somebody who wore his social conscience on his sleeve. Due to his keen interest in financial opportunities, Schiller is fairly certain that Steve Warner would have ended up quite rich.

Both members of Gettysburg College's historical honor society, Schiller and Warner were students in Professor Charles Glatfelter's honors seminar in historical method. The class required a great deal of reading and featured a three-hour discussion group in which the students articulated their views on what they read. Glatfelter recalls Steve as one of the most thorough, inquisitive and well-prepared students of the 6,100 he taught between 1949 and 1989. He noted that:

> In the several classes we had together, he was the student most likely to make statements and ask questions which a teacher would expect from a thoroughly seasoned colleague. Steve did this in a way which made me look forward to the next class with him...[33]

Steve's college career was highly successful. He graduated magna cum laude, with departmental honors in history and was elected to the Phi Beta Kappa honorary

---

[31] *The Gettysburgian,* March 1, 1968.
[32] Letter to the author dated August 14, 2002.
[33] Letter to the author, August 14, 2002.

society. During college, he maintained his interest in a very broad range of subjects. As a junior, the history department awarded Steve a prize for being the student with the highest marks in his field. Steve chose an illustrated architectural study of the Ise Shrine in Japan. He acquired at least some of his interest in Asia from Gettysburg professor Roger Stemen. Mike Hobor, a fellow student, describes Stemen as "a gifted and inspiring teacher of Chinese and Asian history."

Steve decided to pursue his post-graduate education in law school. He desperately wanted to attend Yale in New Haven, Connecticut, which was and is the most selective law school in the country. To be accepted at Yale, a student generally needed not only close to a straight "A" average in undergraduate school but a score on the law school aptitude test (LSAT) in the neighborhood of 700 (99% percentile).[34] Due to the fact that it was one-third the size of Harvard's law school, Yale was much harder to get into. During his senior year, Steve applied to, and was accepted to law school at Yale, Duke and the University of Chicago. Not surprisingly, he chose Yale.

1968--A Year of Trauma

On March 16, 1968, in the wake of the Tet Offensive and Eugene McCarthy's surprising showing in the New Hampshire primary, Senator Robert Kennedy, the late President's brother, announced that he would seek the Democratic Party nomination for President. With the Kennedy candidacy, President Johnson's renomination no longer was certain. Faced with his rapidly diminishing popularity, the President surprised the American public on March 31, when he announced at the end of a televised address to the nation about Vietnam that he would not seek another term as President. Immediately, a spirited contest for the nomination began between McCarthy, Kennedy and Vice-President Hubert Humphrey.

Both Kennedy and McCarthy opposed continuing the War; however, McCarthy accused Kennedy of opportunism--i.e., not challenging Johnson until it was clear that it would be profitable to do so. Humphrey tried without much success to walk a fine line on the War, afraid to break with Johnson, while trying not to alienate those in his party who wanted the American commitment in Vietnam to end immediately.

In the Republican side, former Vice-President Richard Nixon was busily cashing in on all the favors he had performed for Republican candidates and party officials over the last eight years. It soon became apparent that only Nixon could bridge the gap between the ultra conservatives and the rest of the party. While most of the public's attention was focused on the dramatic battle for the Democratic nomination, Nixon was locking up the nomination on the Republican side.

Only five days after Lyndon Johnson announced his withdrawal from the presidential race, another calamity rocked the American body politic. On April 4, while in Memphis, Tennessee to assist African-American garbage collectors in their strike

---

[34] The test is now scored on a scale of 120 to 180. A 700 LSAT score in 1967 would correlate to a current score above 170--almost impossible for a mere mortal to attain.

against the city, the acknowledged leader of the civil rights movement, 39 year-old, Dr. Martin Luther King, Jr., was assassinated. A sniper shot him while he stood with colleagues on the balcony of the motel at which he was staying. Upon learning of King's death, black youths in cities all over the United States rioted. In some cities they looted and burned substantial portions of the inner cities in which they lived.

In white America, even amongst those sympathetic with the message of non-violence espoused by Dr. King,[35] the primary necessity was deemed to be a return to the rule of law and order. The rioters thus played into the hands of the candidates who promised to accomplish that, Richard Nixon and the third-party candidate, the racist governor of Alabama, George Corley Wallace.

The possibility that the 1968 election would become a referendum on the war ended on June 5, when Robert Kennedy was assassinated by a Palestinian, Sirhan Sirhan, after winning the Democratic Party's primary in California.[36] In August, Vice President Humphrey won the Democratic nomination in Chicago, while the city's police battled anti-war demonstrators outside the convention hall.

At the Republican convention the same month, a little excitement was provided by the possibility that the most conservative members of the party, particularly in the South, might abandon Nixon in favor of California Governor Ronald Reagan. Reagan left no doubts where he stood on Vietnam. He told the Republican platform committee that he favored a "stand-firm, fight-to-win position in Vietnam." He proclaimed that it was in America's national interest to do so.[37]

Nixon provided a statement to the platform committee which was a model of ambiguity. He didn't want to alienate the voters who were beginning to tire of the war, but he was more afraid to alienate the right wing of his party. Any showing of a lack of resolve might cause the people who tended to contribute money and work for the ticket to sit on their hands. Nixon attributed his 1962 defeat in the race for governor of California to a lack of enthusiasm for his candidacy on the Republican right. He would make sure that they worked hard to recapture the White House in 1968.

The statement had something for everyone. Nixon called for a new strategy for permitting a phasing out of American troops and a negotiated settlement. He neither explained what this new strategy might be nor what new terms he might offer the Communists. In fact, for four years he would offer North Vietnam nothing but the opportunity to withdraw their forces from South Vietnam. The former Vice-President did not tell the platform committee or the American people that, if the North Vietnamese did not accept such terms, the war would continue indefinitely.

---

[35] A vocal opponent of the Vietnam War.

[36] In their debates during the primary season, Senators McCarthy and Kennedy battled over which was more supportive of Israel, in an effort to curry favor with Jewish voters. Assumedly, this motivated Sirhan to murder Kennedy.

[37] *The New York Times,* August 1, 1968, 20:1.

Further, Nixon told the committee that "the war must be ended...honorably, consistent with the long-term requirements of peace in Asia." He did not explain that a honorable peace was one in which the United States guaranteed the survival of the Saigon government, an objective that could only be achieved by the indefinite presence of large numbers of American soldiers in Vietnam.

Finally, Nixon promised to wage the war with fewer men and at less cost.[38] He did not explain how an honorable peace, i.e., the survival of South Vietnam could be achieved with fewer soldiers than the half million who could not fulfill this objective. Once elected he would convince a large segment of the American population that the South Vietnamese Army, which could not hold its own against the Communists, even with the help of 500,000 American troops, could do so by itself. Indeed, virtually everything that occurred in Vietnam between 1960 and 1975 indicated that this was not so.

Weakened by the dissension in the Democratic Party, occasioned by the Vietnam War, Vice-President Humphrey trailed Richard Nixon badly in the opinion polls conducted in September. Wallace and his running mate, former Air Force General Curtis LeMay, drained support from both candidates. While racists from both parties were attracted to Wallace, many extreme hawks were attracted to the third-party ticket by LeMay's suggestion that the United States bomb North Vietnam "back to the Stone Age."

As the campaign progressed, many Democrats with reservations about Hubert Humphrey returned to the fold, but in the end Nixon was elected. Although he received 301 electoral votes, as opposed to 191 for Humphrey and 46 for Wallace, the popular vote was much closer. Only 43.4 percent of the electorate voted for Nixon; 42.7 percent for Humphrey and 13 percent for Wallace.

On January 20, 1969, Richard M. Nixon became President of the United States. Many, if not most, Americans hoped and believed that he would bring the Vietnam War to a quick conclusion, as Eisenhower had done in Korea in 1953. However, the War continued another four years with more than 20,000 American, and countless thousands of additional Vietnamese, dead.

Universal Draft Avoidance

The process, by which an individual ended up in Vietnam, and most at risk as an infantryman in Vietnam, was serendipitous. As noted by *The Encyclopedia of the Vietnam War:*[39]

> Vietnam was the experience of the generation, but few actually participated directly. This contrasts with the World War II generation, in which virtually all able-bodied men, and a large number of women,

---

[38] *The New York Times,* August 2, 1968, 1.
[39] Spencer C. Tucker, ed., (1998)

entered the services. Through the Korean War years and for several years after, roughly 70 percent of draft-age males served in the military.

The contrast between the level of participation in World War II and Vietnam are startling. In *Chance and Circumstance: the Draft, the War, and the Vietnam Generation*,[40] Lawrence M. Baskir and William A. Strauss provide the following statistics: 26,800,000 American men were of draft age between the time of the Tonkin Gulf resolution on August 4, 1964 and the withdrawal of the last American forces from Vietnam on March 28, 1973. Almost 16 million of these men never served in the military. Of the over 10 million who served in the military, 2.3 million served prior to August 1964. Of the 8.6 million who served during the Vietnam era, 6.4 million never went to Vietnam.[41] As Baskir and Strauss note, out of 27 million men potentially at risk to serve in Vietnam, 25 million did not do so.

Of the approximately 2,000,000 American men who served in Vietnam between 1964 and 1973, Baskir and Strauss state that 550,000 were non-combatants and 1.6 million were combatants. This percentage of combatants strikes me as high and is inconsistent with often cited statistics that for every combat soldier in Vietnam there were several in the rear, maybe as many as six. Of course, some soldiers served time in the field and then were transferred to rear echelon positions. Also, these figures depend on how one defines combat. Were sailors who were stationed on aircraft carriers off the coast of Vietnam combat veterans? What about airmen loading bombs onto planes at relatively secure airbases inside Vietnam or the signal corps personnel, clerks and cooks at a base camp? On the other hand, one might classify a helicopter dust-off crew as support personnel, rather than combat soldiers--regardless of the fact that their jobs could be very dangerous.

In 1970, Steve Warner estimated the number of "grunts," combat infantrymen, at 50-60,000, out of the approximately 400,000 U.S. soldiers in Vietnam--almost 100 percent of which he opined were draftees. He noted that his friend, Jerry Pickering, didn't think that there was "a single lifer" (a career soldier) in his company.[42] In February 1970, the Defense Department (DOD) announced that 12,000 draftees had been killed in Vietnam as of that date, 33 percent of all combat deaths.

One of every 104 men drafted between June 1965 and June 1969 died in Vietnam. *The New York Times* reported that, "[i]n the Army...one of every two soldiers who have died in combat have been draftees." *The Times* noted that draftees were more likely than nondraftees to be combat infantrymen and opined that, as the war lengthened, this trend was likely to become more pronounced. In contrast to the Army, only 5 percent of the

---

[40] Alfred A. Knopf, 1978.

[41] Baskir and Strauss note that 250,000 women served in the military during the Vietnam era; 6,431 served in Vietnam, nine of whom died there. Only one of these, Lt. Sharon Lane, was a victim of hostile fire. Most of the others died in aircraft crashes. Fifty-nine female civilians also lost their lives in Vietnam, http://grunt.space.swri.edu/womenkil/htm.

[42] Gettysburg Collection, Steven Warner's notebook # 17, entry of June 25, 1970.

Marines were draftees; 520 of these involuntary Marines had been killed in combat as of the release of the DOD report.[43]

Most of the 58,000 soldiers who died in Vietnam and the approximately 270,000 who were wounded were among the unlucky few who failed to escape combat after a winnowing out process. Particularly after the Tet offensive, there were precious few true volunteers in Vietnam and very few soldiers who believed that the security of their nation depended on the presence of any American soldiers in Vietnam. Many who went to Vietnam after 1968 did so simply because they believed that they had a duty to go if their government required them to do so--regardless of the reason. Many others went to Vietnam simply because they had no better alternative.

There were many avenues of escape, and the great majority of those who died in Vietnam, certainly by 1969, were those who had failed to avail themselves of these avenues. Claims by some conservative apologists that most of the troops fighting in Vietnam were volunteers, are demonstratively false when talking about the period after 1968; if such claims are true for any period.

While much attention and malice was and is still directed to those who illegally avoided the draft, by such means as fleeing to Canada or Sweden, millions of young Americans avoided military service by perfectly legal means and millions more decreased their chances of combat in Vietnam to the infinitesimal.

Up until 1968, many young men with enough intelligence, fortitude and money to do so could avoid the draft by simply staying in school until they were 26. Some draft boards deferred young men in certain professions indefinitely even after 1968. One of my college roommates dropped out law school to teach and thus was never called by his draft board. Some draft boards deferred young men in the Peace Corps and domestic anti-poverty programs; others did not. In February 1970, Donald Rumsfeld,[44] then head of the Office of Economic Opportunity, announced that his agency would no longer request draft deferments for VISTA (Volunteers In Service To America) volunteers. Standards for hardship deferments also varied from draft board to draft board and were also subject to vagaries of influence peddling. 2.4 million men acquired such deferments during the Vietnam era.[45]

Many young men avoided military service by getting a medical deferment. People with obvious disqualifying impairments, such as blindness, were classified 4-F. However, many young men with more minor impairments were classified 1-Y and were never drafted. Baskir and Strauss state that 5 million young men failed either Selective Service's pre-induction or induction physical examination. While some of these were people who would have been classified 4-F even in World War II, many were so classified due to moderate cases of asthma, allergies, marginally high blood pressure and

---

[43] *The New York Times,* February 12, 1970, 12:4.

[44] As of this writing the Secretary of Defense, a post Rumsfeld also held in the administration of President Gerald Ford in 1975-76.

[45] Baskir and Strauss, p. 27

athletic injuries. As to the latter, there appeared to be an obvious anomaly that someone like New York Jets quarterback Joe Namath, for example, was healthy enough to play professional football, but was unfit for military service

Baskir and Strauss state that the percentage of draft registrants rejected for physical reasons jumped from 37 percent in 1967 to 58 percent in 1973.[46] Since after 1968 more of the potential inductees were better educated and more affluent, one would think that they would have been healthier than those examined in 1967, rather than more infirm. The increase in registrants failing their draft physical was not an accident. Indeed, the more education a registrant had, they more likely he was to fail his physical. This was only in part due to the fact that the more affluent one was, the more likely he was to be able to document a potentially disqualifying condition. On October 11, 1970, *The New York Times* reported:[47]

> No longer able to avoid the military by entering graduate school or draft deferrable occupations, a growing number of young men have found physical disqualification a painless alternative to being drafted, going to jail or leaving the country.

> Usually, these men are aided by private doctors who write letters for them documenting genuine, exaggerated or, in a few instances, fabricated medical conditions.

> Noel Perrin, a Dartmouth College English professor...estimates that 60 percent of the men in the college who have taken the Army physical examination have been permanently disqualified from the military.

> One day last spring, for instance, 34 of 43 Dartmouth students who took the bus to Manchester, N.H., for their pre-induction examinations were disqualified.

There was also tremendous variation as to how those seeking a medical exemption were received at the Armed Forces Examining Stations, particularly as the Vietnam War became increasing unpopular. Baskir and Strauss say:

> At the Boston examination site, for example, graduate students from Harvard and MIT were told, "If you cooperate with us, we'll cooperate with you."

In October 1970, Selective Service Director Curtis Tarr gave *The Times* the following revealing statistics. While 24.2 percent of registrants had failed their physical in 1966, that number had risen to 32.5 percent by the end of June 1970. For July 1970, the failure rate was 40.7 percent. Tarr's statistics also defied the conventional wisdom that Caucasians tend to be healthier than blacks on account of their generally greater affluence. In July 1970, 41.5 percent of white registrants failed their physical, compared with 32.4 percent for blacks.

---

[46] Ibid.
[47] Page 1:8.

This comports with my recollection of encountering a busload of Harvard graduate students returning from their pre-induction physical at the Boston Army Base, in which virtually none passed. By contrast, when I took my pre-induction physical in Richmond, Virginia, in the summer of 1967, everyone who walked into the examining station under his own power passed.

My recollections in this regard are confirmed by Curtis Tarr's statistics. In 1969, 45.7 percent of those taking their pre-induction physical in Massachusetts failed. In New York, 42.3 percent failed. The comparable figures for South Carolina and Georgia were 17.9 percent and 27 percent respectively.

Baskir and Strauss also state that in the later years of the Vietnam War, examiners at the Seattle examining station gave an exemption to everyone who had a physician's note, regardless of what it said. In some places, at least some young men were given medical exemptions on the basis of physicians' letters without even having to report to an Armed Forces examining station. At Richmond, Virginia, in 1967, by contrast, every physician's letter was examined by the Army doctors with a jaundiced eye.

Some potential inductees were able to artificially manipulate their blood pressure in order to fail the pre-induction physical. Army physicians, aware that this could be done with drugs, kept one young man at the Fort Belvoir hospital for three days in 1970. They wanted to see whether his blood pressure would drop if they kept him in a controlled environment. By staying awake for three days, drinking coffee and constantly starting arguments about the war with other young men, this individual was able to keep his blood pressure above that level that disqualified him for military service.

However, while the easy medical exemption was a very popular means of draft avoidance in some areas, one of the surest ways to make certain you would never go to Vietnam was to join the Reserves or National Guard. Once the draft rules changed in 1968, there was another mad rush into the reserve and guard. It was generally understood that due to the outcry when President Kennedy called up the National Guard during the Berlin crisis of 1961, President Johnson would never do the same thing. In 1966, *Life* magazine described the reserves and guard as "traditional sanctuaries from the draft."[48]

Richard Todd, a reservist on his way to his two-2 week summer camp at Ft. Dix, in 1969, wrote a contemporaneous view of what motivated most reservists and guardsman in an article in *The New York Times Magazine* of October 12, 1969, entitled, "Life With the Conscientious Acceptors."

> ...like a lobster pot, the Reserves mean one thing to those on top and another to those who exist uneasily below. What lures almost everyone who joins the Reserves is the promise of a part-time career free of violence, pain or much obligation. Whatever their strategic value, the chief function of the Reserves to reservists is to shelter them from the draft. During the past four years of high

---

[48] *Life*, Vol. 61, No. 24, December 9, 1966.

draft calls, competition for a spot in the Reserves has been intense. To enlist, applicants take the useful Armed Forces Qualification Test, and some attention is paid to their score, but a timely arrival and a friend in the back room may mean more. It has often been rumored that unit commanders were selling enlistments for as much as $1,200. I have never met anyone who admitted to buying his way in; on the other hand, plenty of people say it would have been worth a thousand to them at the time. Almost anyone here can tell you how many days he had left, before getting his induction notice, when his Reserve spot came through.

...the majority of reservists are the draftable young men who sign up for a six-year term of service....This begins with a short period of [active duty]....In most cases it is only four months: eight weeks of basic training, eight weeks of specialized school--cook's, clerk's, infantryman's, etc. Then the reservist reverts to inactive status, and serves out the remaining five and a half years in quiet weekend meetings and summer camps.

Or so he hopes. There is, of course, always the threat of "call-up" a word reservists find as unpleasant to pronounce as "cancer." About 37,000 men have been mobilized since the start of the long war. This was fewer than almost anyone predicted, but it shivered the fortunate majority.[49]

In the Korean War, 700,000 guardsmen and reservists were called to active duty; during the 1961 Berlin crisis: 140,000. By late 1969, there were 750,000 army reserve and national guard troops on the rolls; 37,000 were activated in 1968, in part due to North Korea's capture of the U.S. Navy ship *The Pueblo*.[50] No guardsmen or reservists were activated before or after 1968. Only 15,000 of those activated went to Vietnam.[51]

To obtain a place in the guard or the reserves without connections required some effort. Few blacks found refuge from the draft in these components. A Wayne State University study in 1969, characterized the National Guard as, "a haven for white draft dodgers."[52] The Guard, not surprisingly, vigorously denied this.

If a young man tried to find a place in the guard units in big cities, he was unlikely to be successful. Several Harvard Law School classmates of mine traveled all over New England looking for openings and found some in a New Hampshire unit of signal corps "pole-climbers." Another classmate traveled all over the South until he found an opening in a unit in Mississippi. Since each National Guard Unit was responsible for filling its ranks, there were many opportunities to obtain the coveted spots

---

[49] *The New York Times Magazine,* October 12, 1969, VII: 27, quoted by permission of *The New York Times* and Richard Todd.
[50] Ibid., Richard Todd's figure for Korean call-ups is 938,000; The 700,000 figure is from Baskir and Strauss.
[51] Amongst the unluckiest people during the Vietnam War, considering the odds against it, were the relatively few guardsmen and reservists killed in Vietnam. Among these were several members of a Bardstown, Kentucky, artillery unit who died when Communist forces attacked their fire support base in June 1969.
[52] *The New York Times,* January 5, 1969, 76:1.

through influence peddling and even bribery. As early as 1965 there were long waiting lists of applicants for many National Guard units. A recruiting sergeant for a New York unit who took advantage of this market was arrested for asking for a $200 pay-off to enroll New York Jets player Bob Schweickert.[53]

Indeed, the National Football League, so inclined to drape itself in the flag, is one of best examples of how important connections could be in obtaining one of the coveted spots in a reserve or National Guard unit. The NFL never stopped publicizing the stories of players like the Pittsburgh Steelers' Rocky Blier, who was wounded in Vietnam, because so few of its players served in the war. This was not an accident.

On December 9, 1966, in an issue about the inequities of the draft and draft avoidance, *Life* magazine devoted several pages to the NFL.[54] The article was entitled "Bald Case in Point: Pro Football's Magical Immunity."

Of all the occupational groups subject to Selective Service, none has worked out a more effective immunity than professional football. In 1966, 27 percent of the entire available U.S. manpower pool (1-A's between the age of 18 and 35) was drafted. It is not known how many of the 960 players in the two football leagues are actually 1-A. But the fact is that only two big league players have been drafted--and even with them it was close.

The pros have acquired their immunity by managing to get placed in reserve and guard units....Reserve and Guard units, which are unlikely to be activated under present conditions are the safest haven. The only hitch is getting the players into these units which frequently have long waiting lists.

Noting how anxious pro football teams were to protect their investment in each player, *Life* observed:

Nearly every team has a front-office military affairs specialist....As the draft board closes in, this man sees that the threatened player applies for membership in a Guard or reserve outfit. Unit commanders, who are often fans themselves, are happy to sign up the football players, often leapfrogging them over the waiting list. Ordinary citizens have to sweat out their turn and run the risk of being drafted while they wait.

Major General George Gelson, Jr., of the Maryland National Guard, was quoted as saying:

We have an arrangement with the Colts [then in Baltimore], when they have a player with a military problem, they send him to us.[55]

---

[53] *The New York Times,* December 3, 1965, p. 1.
[54] *Life, Vol. 61, No. 24, pp. 44-46; copyright 1966 TIME Inc. quoted by permission.*
[55] *Ibid.*

Life reported that 10 Dallas Cowboy players were assigned to the headquarters unit of a Texas National Guard unit and five Washington Redskins players were assigned to a similar unit in D.C. One of the two unlucky players who were drafted, was Cardinals [then in St. Louis] quarterback Gary Snook. Snook was inducted because his rather atypical draft board ignored the pleas of the Cardinals' management to delay his induction until the team could obtain a reserve or guard slot for him.

Of course, pro football players were not the only young men to be shown preference in obtaining a place in bosom of the National Guard or Reserves. The sons of prominent men fared much better than those without connections. According to Myra McPherson, in *Long Time Passing,* of the 234 sons of United States Senators and Congressmen who turned 18 during the Vietnam War, [56]only 28 served in Vietnam, ten of whom saw combat, and only one of whom was wounded.

If a young man failed to secure a medical exemption or a slot in the National Guard or Reserves, he could almost assuredly avoid Vietnam combat by enlisting in the Navy or Air Force. While 38,000 U.S. Army personnel and approximately 15,000 servicemen from the much smaller U.S. Marine Corps died in Vietnam, the numbers for the Navy and the Air Force are about 2,500 each.[57] Moreover, most of the Navy and Air Force casualties were pilots. The sailors of the "Brown Water Fleet" instituted by the Navy to patrol the inland waterways of Vietnam were exceptions to this rule. Some of these veterans joined the Navy to avoid combat in Vietnam and were foiled by their service's insistence on getting a piece of the action on the ground.

To be a Navy or Air Force veteran of Vietnam is generally a very different thing from being a Navy or Army Corps veteran of World War II. Many enlisted men in the Air Corps died in the Second World War. The American bombers that flew over Germany and Nazi-occupied territory often consisted of crews of eight, many of whom died when their planes were shot down and some who died from shrapnel wounds even when their planes made it back to England or Italy.[58]

One Air Force recruiter lost his job in 1970 by being candid and selling his service as a low-risk alternative to the Army. Tech. Sergeant Robert W. Knapp, a recruiter in Meriden, Connecticut, was fired for sending potential recruits a letter that stated the following:

> Did you know that the vast majority of the U.S. forces killed in Southeast Asia have been draftees? Wouldn't you rather take advantage of the opportunity to join the branch of service that has lost the least amount of men in Southeast Asia, as opposed to being drafted into the branch of the service that has lost the most?

---

[56] One of which was Albert Gore, Jr., the son of one of Tennessee's senators; another was George W. Bush, the oldest son of Congressman George H. W. Bush of Texas.

[57] http://www.archives.gov/research_room/research_topics/vietnam_war_casualty_lists/statistics.html #cause

[58] Towards the end of the Vietnam War, the North Vietnamese shot down a number of B-52s over Hanoi and Haiphong, killing a number of enlisted crewmembers, as well as pilots.

Are you willing to take this gamble with your life or would you rather go into a branch of service that will train you to be a better citizen, a service that is virtually noncombatant?[59]

While being a sailor was generally much safer than being a soldier even in World War II, the Japanese and Germans were able to sink many American ships and kill approximately 37,000 Navy personnel. When the enemy succeeded, their success was often spectacular with gruesome results--as when the Japanese sank the U.S.S. Indianapolis in 1945, with the loss of 883 sailors, many of whom it is suspected were eaten by sharks.

The downside to enlisting in the Navy or Air Force during the Vietnam War was that the term of enlistment was four years, rather than the two years one would serve if drafted. Officer Candidate Programs in the Navy and Air Force became very difficult to get into after 1968, and four years as an enlisted man--particularly for college graduates, was not that appealing an alternative to the draft. I recall encountering a college-educated Air Force enlisted man in Saigon who was teaching English to Vietnamese non-commissioned officers who were not trying very hard to learn. He expressed regret at not taking his chances with the draft.

The alternative of long-term service as an enlisted man was one of the few avenues of escape from the draft that favored those with a high school degree but not a college degree. Four years in the Air Force or Navy would have been more appealing and beneficial to one without a college degree, because the alternative opportunities in the civilian economy during those four years were not much better than what the military had to offer.

The Army was also willing to negotiate a deal with those threatened by the draft. If a young man was willing to enlist for three years instead of two, the army recruiters said he would be sent to the occupational schooling of his choice. Thus, as the Army conceded, in exchange for an extra year of your life, you could greatly increase your chances of surviving your military service.

A spokesman of the Defense Department denied there was a deliberate policy of sending more draftees into infantry positions. But army officials said that the process of selection, which allows volunteers to choose their type of work, was unfavorable to draftees.[60]

Other young men enlisted for two years under the assumption that this would also give some preference in the job to which the Army would assign them. Others enlisted

---

[59] *The New York Times,* June 5, 1970, 7:1. Sgt. Knapp was not the only Air Force recruiter to sell his service as a sanctuary from the Army. In September 1963, before the Vietnam build-up, a recruiter for the Air Force ROTC unit at Miami University predicted that high draft calls would recur, and that, I would then rue the day that I spurned his solicitation. He turned out to be quite prescient.
[60] *The New York Times,* February 12, 1970, 12:4.

because they assumed they would be drafted in any event and decided to put an end to the uncertainty and anxiety of waiting for the axe to fall. Statistics on the number of "volunteers" in Vietnam are very misleading since many who enlisted, including junior officers, did so only because they expected to be drafted. Without the draft, the vast majority of these men, particularly after 1968, would not have been in the military. The number who would have volunteered for service in Vietnam after 1968 without the prodding of compulsion is infinitesimal.

Once a soldier was assigned to a combat specialty it was very difficult to get transferred to a non-combat position or training in a non-combat military occupational specialty. Generally, a soldier assigned Advanced Infantry Training after Basic Training was stuck, aware of the fact that he was now a member of a select group with the highest likelihood of being killed in Vietnam. Although the Army was reluctant to make changes after a soldier had orders to Advanced Training, there were exceptions. On my way to Fort Lewis, Washington, for shipment to Vietnam, I met another soldier who was on his way to Korea. He had been drafted and assigned to Advanced Infantry School upon completing basic training. He immediately went to the Army recruiter on post and asked to enlist for three years in exchange for assignment to a different training program. The recruiter agreed and asked him which program he wanted. My friend responded, "a MOS (military occupational specialty) that they can't use in Vietnam." The recruiter had his orders changed, assigning him to training as a nuclear weapons repairman.

Steve Warner was stripped of his student deferment and was reclassified as "1-A," immediately available for induction into the Armed Forces, almost as soon as he graduated in June 1968. He apparently did not make any effort to get into a National Guard or Reserve Unit, or to obtain a 1-Y physical exemption. Reporting for his pre-induction physical examination on July 2, Steve was one of only ten young men, out of one hundred from his draft board, who was found physically fit for military service after the initial examination.[61]

Steve and his father did discuss the possibility of enlisting in one of the Armed Services at length. They also discussed whether Steve should leave the country and go to Canada or Sweden. Steve decided not to avoid the draft by illegal means. A college friend, Michael Hobor, believes that Steve's decisions regarding the draft were fueled to some extent by his plans for the future:

> I think Steven had political ambitions and wanted to run for office some day. He was very much a part of his times and believed 'he could make a difference and make things better'---'if I had the power.' It is my firm belief that this was an important motivation for him as he entered military service. In other words, he went into the military perhaps in part because he sensed no alternative, but also because he saw it as vital to any political ambitions he had. From our perspective as the sons of men who had fought in WWII, it was inconceivable that someone could expect to be trusted with public office if he had not put on a uniform when

---

[61] July 1968 letter from Stephen Warner to Susan Walsky.

the country was at war, even if unhappy with the war itself. Steven would never have "done a Clinton."[62]

However, on advice of some of his father's friends, Steve decided to try to delay his induction by appealing his reclassification. His objective was to get through the fall semester at Yale Law School, noting that "even one semester at Yale will make me into a mini-expert on Selective Service and military law."[63]

On July 12, 1968, Steve Warner wrote Professor Stemen at Gettysburg about his predicament:

> Like most of the senior males, I have been reclassified 1A and expect my induction notice in the early fall, though with appeals, etc., I can probably squeeze in at least one semester of law school.

Selective Service regulations provided that a young man who was reclassified could request a personal appearance before his draft board. The local draft board would then rule on his request for further deferment. Following notification of the draft board's decision, the individual could appeal its decision to a state appeals board. The appeals board decision could take several months. Curiously, although a student had to appear in person before his local draft board, he could have his appeal transferred to the state in which he was attending graduate school. This was so despite the fact that the appeal was determined solely on the basis on documents.

Yale Law School

Steve was able to complete not only a semester, but a full year at Yale by exhausting the appeals procedure.[64] While in Steve's case, the delay made no difference to the outcome of his military service, it may well have been crucial for others. 1969 was a much bloodier year for American troops in Vietnam than was 1970. 9,414 GIs were killed in action in the former year; 4,221 in the latter. Approximately 2,000 soldiers died in "non hostile" incidents in both years. Moreover, given the greater need of combat

---

[62] Email to author, August 19, 2002. I have often wondered why Bill Clinton, who decided he was going to be President as a teenager, did not serve in the military to protect his future political credentials. He had sufficient connections even in 1969 to assure that he would never see combat. I submit that "doing a Clinton" was no more dishonorable than the conduct of millions of other young men at the time.

[63] July 1968 letter to Susan Walsky.

[64] This author delayed his induction by following a similar path. I was reclassified 1-A in August 1968. I appeared before my local draft board in Arlington, Virginia, in October 1968. I recall going home and watching the seventh game of the 1968 World Series afterwards. Upon receiving my local draft board's rejection of my request for further deferment, I had my appeal transferred to Massachusetts, where I was attending law school. In February 1969, I was informed that my appeal had been rejected and I received a notice for induction dated February 25, ordering me to report to my draft board for induction on March 12, 1969. The notice advised me that I would be allowed to postpone my induction until the end of the current semester, but that no further postponements would be allowed. I was inducted on June 26, three weeks after the last examination of my second year of law school. That night, I arrived with 47 other young men from Arlington and Alexandria, Virginia, at Fort Dix, New Jersey. Stephen Warner had arrived at Fort Dix on June 3, three weeks earlier.

troops in 1968 and 1969, those of us who went to Vietnam in 1970 and enjoyed the life of Riley in the rear, might well have had a different experience if we had served just a little bit earlier.

After a brief and unsuccessful try at being a salesman, Steve started a summer job in 1968 at the South Street Seaport Museum in New York City. The Museum was planning to open a recreation of a 19th century wholesale tea shop. Steve had been assigned to prepare a bibliography regarding the tea trade in New York, gather material and write a background paper on the subject and collect material for physically recreating the shop. He sent Professor Stemen a draft of an outline for his paper and asked for a critique and suggestions for where he might find source material.

Steve also spent a lot of time studying and investing in the stock market. He wrote to his friend Susan Walsky in July 1968, "Del Webb is behaving marvelously this week, or at least on Monday and Tuesday. It isn't every week you make $4,000 in two days, even if it is only on paper. A million by 35."

In September, Steve traveled to New Haven, Connecticut and became a member of the Yale Law School Class of 1971. To his friend Susan Walsky, he confided, "my god everyone is so intelligent. How did I ever get here and more to the point, how am I ever going to stay?" He observed that "everyone is in awe of everyone else until you get a rather crazy self-enforcing circle of awe going."[65]

Steve's professors were all very prominent names in the legal profession. James William Moore, who taught him Federal Court Procedure, was the author of the standard treatise on the subject, recognized as authoritative even by the United States Supreme Court. Guido Calabresi, who was Steve's Torts[66] professor, later became the Dean of the Yale Law School and then a United States Court of Appeals Judge. Thomas Emerson, his Constitutional Law Professor, was a highly regarded expert on the First Amendment to the United States Constitution. For Contracts, Steve had one of the first female professors at the Yale Law School, Ellen Peters, later Chief Justice of the Connecticut Supreme Court.

Like most first-year law students, Steve grappled with the very different technique employed by law school professors as compared with college professors. The student reads assigned cases, the point of which are not always readily apparent. In class, law professors generally do not lecture, they teach their courses by asking the students questions about the cases they just read. Some professors call on students, rather than relying on volunteers. Those students who are not fully prepared often endure a most unpleasant inquisition. After asking about an assigned case, the professor often asks some more questions with slightly different fact patterns. While some students catch on

---

[65] Along these lines, another Yale Law School graduate commented to me that the value of attending Yale Law School was that it "demystified" the place for him. Another friend, a Harvard Law School graduate, observed that the value of going to Harvard Law School was not having to be impressed by people who also went there.

[66] A tort is an injury to another person or another person's property for which one can be sued for damages, such as injuries caused by one's negligence in driving an automobile.

quickly, others spend much of their law school careers feeling as if they just walked into the middle of a movie.

Basic Training 1969

On June 3, 1969, Steve was inducted into the U.S. Army and sent to Fort Dix, New Jersey. From time immemorial, few things in human experience are quite so stark as the transition from being a civilian to being a soldier. Thomas Wentworth Higginson, who enlisted in the Union Army in 1862, observed:[67]

> It was a day absolutely broken off from all that had gone before it. To say that it brought a sense of utter novelty, is nothing; the transformation seemed as perfect, as if, by some suddenly revealed process, one had learned to swim in air, and were striking out for some new planet. The past was annihilated, the future was all.[68]

Typically, the day began by reporting early in the morning to the draft board. Inductees were then bussed to an Armed Forced Induction Station, where a final physical examination was administered. At some point, the men were sworn into the United States Army, although on occasion, including parts of June of 1969, a few men were drafted into the United States Marine Corps. Unlike their World War II counterparts, draftees during the Vietnam era were never assigned to the Navy or Air Force (Air Corps in World War II). Due to the fact that service in the Navy and Air Force was generally much safer than service in the Army or Marines, the former had no need for conscripts.

Afterwards, the inductees were transported to an Army Basic Training Base. A typical stay at Fort Dix began with being ushered into a courtyard where uniforms were distributed by soldiers, who screamed constantly at the new arrivals. To the uninitiated, these men appeared to be sergeants, but in fact were more likely privates who had been in the Army only weeks longer than the objects of their derision. The newly-arrived soldiers were essentially treated like convicts. Either the first night or soon thereafter, they were subjected to a "shakedown" in which screaming cadre had them empty out their duffel-bags to search for weapons, drugs and pornography.

For about a week, new inductees remained in a reception station where they were subjected to a battery of tests, which in some cases determined their fate. One of the tests, for example, tested aptitude for learning the Morse Code. The soldiers sat for an hour with earphones on listening to two or three Morse symbols, which they recorded on a sheet of paper. Some of those who performed well ultimately were sent for training in Signal Corps specialties--thus sparing them from the infantry. Other tests measured clerical or mechanical skills. Another highlight in the week at the reception station was the administration of the Army haircut--which in 1969 was a very dramatic change from the styles worn by civilians.

---

[67] The commander of the first black regiment.
[68] Higginson, from the preface to *The Harvard Memorial Biographies,* 1866.

For anyone who had ever read a story by Franz Kafka, there was a suspicion that he had been trapped in one of Kafka's more disturbing tales. The week at the reception station was marked by constant petty harassment. Digestion was difficult due to the constant screaming at the mess halls. The most familiar refrain was, "Eat up and get out of my mess hall." "Don't just sit there, eat up and get out."

At the end of a week or so at the reception station, new soldiers were assigned to a basic training company--usually, but not always, at the same post. Steve Warner spent eight weeks, from June 16 through August 8, 1969, in A Company, 6th Battalion, 3rd Basic Training Brigade (A-6-3) at Fort Dix. Typically, the initiation upon arrival at the training company was, if anything, more traumatic than that at the reception station. The sergeants and officers often greeted their new charges with constant screaming and threats. Before the first meal (and all subsequent meals), the soldiers lined up in front of an elevated horizontal wooden ladder. They were required to grab the first rung and then, by alternating their hands in grabbing the rest of the fourteen rungs, negotiate the ladder up and back before being allowed to eat. The author had the misfortune of being first in line in front of the ladder for the first evening meal. He failed to notice the step on the side of one of the support columns, and thus was unable to determine how one reached the rungs ten feet above the ground. The sergeants and cooks broke out in derisive laughter, commenting on how this group of trainees was even more stupid than the last one.

College-educated trainees or those with graduate degrees were sometimes singled out for special attention. In one company, the distribution of field equipment was interrupted by the senior sergeant (the field first) who inquired as to which of the 200 soldiers "was the one with all the education." After persistent inquiry, a recent law school graduate was forced to acknowledge the fact that he had "19 years of education." The sergeant then inquired whether the soldier could "walk and chew gum at the same time." He noted that the last trainee with a graduate degree was unable to do so.

At many companies, there was an initiation ceremony soon after the new company began its training. In Fort Dix's B-5-2 (B Company, 5th Battalion, 2nd Brigade), a company training at the same time as Steve Warner's, the ceremony occurred the first full morning at inspection. Sergeants ripped apart each soldier's bed and threw the mattress on the floor, then dumped everything out of the wall and foot lockers onto the floor.

The training portion of basic combat training was, for the most part, incredibly boring, until several weeks passed and the company began to march out to the rifle ranges. Much of the time was spent learning Army drill and ceremony, during which the clock seemed to be running backwards. One learned such useful skills as how to march in step, execute an about-face, salute, hold a rifle at order, port and right shoulder arms. The trainee also endured daily barracks inspections, which included his bunk, wall and foot lockers. At morning formation, the cadre inspected each soldier's uniform including the shine on his boots and belt buckle. Attention was also paid to whether the trainee had a regulation haircut and had shaved. A soldier with a heavy beard was often challenged as to the latter. When assuring the cadre, that I had in fact shaved, this author was often warned "next time stand closer to your razor."

When several weeks had passed, things began to improve, in part because each soldier had become accustomed to the Army way of doing things, in part because the cadre had become satisfied with the psychological pain they had already inflicted. Rising at four or 4:30 a.m., the trainee's day typically started with a mile run in combat boots on a track. However, at Fort Dix during the summer of 1969, the most difficult part of each day was generally a forced march of several miles out to one of the rifle ranges and a forced march back at the end of the day. Occasionally, the troops were treated to a ride in a vehicle referred to as a cattle car. The soldiers were packed in so tightly that one had to place his knees between the knees of the soldier sitting across from him. During the ride, some of the troops actually mooed.

The infantry walk at Fort Dix consisted of sand which made the march, made at a 4 - 5 mile per hour pace, much more strenuous than if it had been over more compact soil. To those who had trouble keeping up with the pace of the march, encouragement was provided by the cadre, most of whom had recently returned from Vietnam--some with painful wounds. Constant berating and an occasional kick were commonplace for the laggards. When the cadre didn't feel up to administering the punishment themselves, they encouraged other trainees to do so. The atmosphere of brutality was enhanced by some of the ditties the troops sang together as they marched. Although some of these tunes were pornographic, others reinforced a degree of contempt for compassion. One of the most common songs was the following lyric:

> A yellow bird with a yellow bill
> He sat upon my windowsill.
> I coaxed him in with a piece of bread
> And then I crushed his fucking head.

None of the marching tunes had anything to do with patriotism or, as in World War II, accomplishing a mission that was necessary. Instead, the tunes evoked personal bravado and fatalism. Among these was the following:

> If I die in a combat zone, box me up and ship me home.

The only one that referred to Vietnam at all went like this:

> I want to be an Airborne Ranger; I want to live a life of danger;
> I want to go to Vietnam; I want to kill some Viet Cong.

In Bravo Company, 5-2 in the summer of 1969, the forced marches were particularly difficult because they were usually led by Sergeant First Class William E. Sapp, a drill sergeant who looked like he had been sent to the company from central casting. Sapp was a 6'3" black man with broad shoulders and a narrow waist. He looked like a professional athlete. Under his drill sergeant's (Smokey the Bear) hat, one could barely see his eyes, but could clearly discern his menacing mustache and intimidating glare. As each one of Sgt. Sapp's strides required three from the average trainee, his forced marches were grueling. One trainee in the company was an overweight National Guardsman who passed out every day during the march to the rifle range. Those in the rear of the column as it marched, were certain to encounter him lying face up in the sand each day, usually within the first mile of the march. Each day there came a point when the column divided to avoid stepping on him.

Marksmanship training was a task the United States Army performed very well in 1969. Intricate safety precautions were taken and reinforced by the noncommissioned officers to insure that the trainees didn't shoot each other either accidentally or on purpose. One of the rules that was constantly driven home, at times with a forceful kick from one of the cadre, was to always have your weapon pointing down range. It was one aspect of Army brutality that every trainee should have appreciated--given the number of his colleagues who were quite capable of accidentally discharging their rifle into the ranks of the people lined up behind his firing position.

It was sometimes quite surprising as to which trainee turned out to be the star of the rifle range. In one company in 1969 at Ft. Bragg, a National Guardsman from New York City, who had never handled a firearm before, could not miss the targets with an M-14. After winning a case of scotch for his drill sergeant with his prowess, he was asked to change shirts with several trainees, who could not hit anything in his company's record fire [final marksmanship test]. Each soldier in basic training was required to hit 30 out of 82 targets to graduate from basic training. The distance to the targets varied greatly. Some of them were relatively close, some as far as 400 yards away. Shots were taken from different positions. The first sixteen were taken from a foxhole, which gave the shooter maximum stability. The next sixteen were taken from a kneeling position, with one elbow supported on a knee. Some shots were taken from a standing position.

The marksmanship of the trainees tended to vary greatly. One had to have incredibly good eye to hand coordination to hit over 65 targets. The average was probably in the 45-55 range. There were some soldiers, however, who fell far short of the 30 targets needed to pass. The sure-shot guardsman agreed to fire only for those trainees who would never end up in Vietnam. He did not want to be responsible if someone ended up in combat and could not defend himself.

In addition to the marksmanship training, the trainees had to endure terribly boring classes on such subjects as first aid, which did include useful instructions on how to carry a wounded comrade; land navigation (reading a compass), hand-to-hand combat (a few basic lessons in karate) and military justice. However, some of these classes were given inside air-conditioned buildings and thus were regarded as a treat, regardless of their content. Members of the cadre constantly perused the audience looking for trainees who might be using the class as an opportunity to catch up on their sleep.

There were some classes, however, that were impossible to sleep through. The drill sergeants and their assistants walked through the ranks during bayonet training to make sure that when they yelled, "what is the spirit of bayonet?" All the trainees responded with "kill, kill, kill!" Steve Warner reported to his parents that once when he stabbed the dummy with his bayonet, his sergeant asked, "Can't you put a little more feeling into it!" The only real combat training was done with pugal sticks, in which trainees protected by a football helmet, facemask and padding tried to beat each other up with padded sticks. In B-5-2 only a few trainees actually fought each other with the sticks.

Basic training also included some instruction and practice in throwing a hand grenade. In many or most companies, most of the training was done with duds; a soldier threw only one live grenade. This was probably the only occasion in which a panic attack could result in the trainee and the supervising cadre being killed. After pulling the pin on the grenade, the trainee had to toss it over a wall, approximately six feet high. Some barely cleared it. If the grenade bounced back, the supervising soldier (often recently back from Vietnam) had to quickly kick it into a pit and hit the pavement in order to avoid being serrated with shrapnel. The cadre in Steve Warner's basic training company had so little confidence in his athletic ability that they wouldn't allow him to throw a live grenade. [69]

The Army also provided training in the use of gas masks. One of the highlights of basic training was being taken into a shed full of tear gas, being forced to remove your gas mask and state your name, rank and serial number before leaving the shed. One was not supposed to run out of the shed, but many trainees could not restrain themselves. The drill sergeants would also, on one or several occasions, toss a tear gas canister into a formation of unsuspecting soldiers to see if they were able to use their gas masks when they weren't expecting to do so.

Basic training also consisted of recurring preparation for the Army physical training test. The PT test consisted of five events. Negotiating a set of overhead parallel bars, low-crawling 40 yards, running a obstacle course (dodge, run and jump), sprinting 150 yards (75 yards up and back) while carrying someone approximately your own weight and a mile run in combat boots.

A perfect score was 500 points. 300 points was passing and those who failed were assumedly doomed to repeat basic training. The minimum average performance that got one to 300 points was 36 seconds for the low crawl; 36 rungs for the overhead ladder; 25 seconds for the run, dodge and jump; approximately 50 seconds for the man carry and 8:33 for the mile. [70] The cadre subjected those trainees who were overweight and unable

---

[69] Gettysburg Notebook 23, entry of May 16, 1970. He got a second chance in training conducted in Vietnam almost a year later.

[70] My source is my own PT card. At times the Army substituted a grenade throw for the run, dodge and jump. This would have greatly enhanced my score in that it replaced my worst event with one in which I excelled.

to score over 300 in practice sessions to merciless harassment.[71] It was not uncommon for some of the trainees to vomit during the PT tests, and sometimes at the end of the forced marches.

The cadre, on the other hand, showed begrudging respect for those who excelled in the PT tests. The maximum score for the overhead ladder was 76 bars (three trips up and back). While most trainees struggled, virtually every company had one or two men, generally small and wiry, who negotiated the 76 bars without breaking a sweat.

Basic training included rudimentary lessons in tactics, essentially teaching that while half the soldiers were firing, others should advance, and vice versa. That way an enemy soldier would not have the luxury of taking his time to aim at the advancing troops. One evening was spent on a night infiltration course. This entailed low-crawling across a sandy field while machine guns fired live ammunition overhead. During a daylight dry run, the exercise appeared to be very dangerous. At night, however, it became obvious from the tracer rounds, that one could get up and run through the course, if the trainee was able to avoid being spotted by one of the cadre. Playing by the rules was most unpleasant, since the dry run generally left one with raw abrasions on the inside of his elbows and knees. During the night-time run, the sand irritated the wounds much more.[72]

There was a large psychological component to basic training. A trainee was essentially deprived of all personal freedom. One had no access to newspapers, thus it was very difficult to stay abreast of what was going on in the outside world. I was aware of the first moon landing on July 20, only because I happened to be on fire guard at the time and could hear one of the cadre listening to the radio down the hall. On the other hand, I did not become aware of Senator Ted Kennedy's automobile accident at Chappaquiddick until some time after it occurred.

Although a few trainees had transistor radios, there was only a very limited opportunity to listen to them. The songs one heard constantly were Neil Diamond's nostalgic "Sweet Caroline," which I associate to this day with basic training, and the very annoying "In the Year 2525."

Fire guard duty was perhaps, next to KP, one of the most difficult tasks to adjust to. Every third night, a trainee was awakened in the middle of the night to stand watch for an hour. One had to be very careful not to sit down, or even lean too long against a wall--for fear of falling asleep. One morning, my company was awakened to the screaming of the drill sergeants and noticed immediately that it was already light outside. The next to last fire guard had fallen asleep and thus his replacement had not awakened

---

[71] On the other hand, the only nice thing SFC Sapp ever said about any trainee in B-5-2 was an expression of respect for the National Guardsman who always passed out on the forced marches. This soldier passed the final PT test with a score of 302. While expressing his contempt for the rest of the company, particularly those who failed the PT test, Sapp acknowledged the fortitude of the guardsman.

[72] Law school friends who had attended a ROTC summer camp, advised this author to buy Kotex and wrap them around the inside of my elbows and knees. They did advise, however, that if I was caught, the consequences were likely to be most unpleasant and lingering.

us at 4:30. However, one understood the necessity of this ordeal and how disastrous such a lapse might be in Vietnam.

There were many other petty annoyances. The cadre used the smokers' habit as a psychological weapon. Often they were allowed to light a cigarette only to be told immediately to put it out again. There was a soda machine at the entrance to the mess hall which cadre, but not trainees, were allowed to use. By depriving the trainees of almost all sweets, the Army helped the overweight trainees lose a considerable amount of weight in eight weeks. Often, however, the cadre had some fun doing this. One day as the trainees of B-5-2 stood in formation in 95 degree heat, Sgt. Ulf Tornbloom had one of them go over to a snack truck parked nearby and buy a large coke filled with ice. Then as the troops watched in agony, Sgt. Tornbloom slowly drank it in front of us.

The basic training experience for the National Guardsman or Reservist was very different from that of the draftee. They knew that after eight miserable weeks, followed by eight slightly less miserable weeks of advanced individual training, they would be going home to resume their normal lives. By 1969, even some college graduate draftees also took much of basic training none too seriously. They assumed that Army would make use of their education and not make infantryman out of them. Those who went through basic training in 1969 turned out to be generally correct on this point. However, if the war had been escalated as certain people in the civilian and military leadership desired, many of these people would have been most unpleasantly surprised and the toll of the Vietnam War would have been quite a bit higher and spread out over more of a spectrum of American society than it was.

Some of the college graduates had decided that, if they were going to serve, they might as well do it as officers, rather than enlisted men. Thus, they had committed themselves to attending officer candidate school (OCS) after completion of basic and advanced individual training. At the completion of the 6-month OCS course, the newly-minted second lieutenant was obligated to two years of active duty. Thus, one practical consequence of committing to OCS, instead of serving two years as an enlisted draftee, was spending an additional ten months in the Army. Worse yet, one could reasonably expect the entire ten-months prior to receiving a commission to be full of the kind of petty harassment that one had to endure in basic.

One the other hand, going to OCS meant that one would not be sent to Vietnam for probably another year, maybe longer. In the summer of 1969, with the war seeming to be winding down, it was not an unreasonable hope that by delaying deployment to Vietnam, one might avoid the war altogether. Given the way troop levels declined in Vietnam in 1970-71, this gamble may have paid off for many that chose the OCS route. However, others ended up serving in Vietnam as late as 1971-72. [73]

---

[73] One of the most bizarre twists of fate I am aware of involves a high school classmate, who upon being drafted in 1968, decided he would become the most proficient soldier the Army could produce. He desperately wanted to go to Vietnam and experience combat. To that end, he became a Special Forces officer. By the time he had completed all his training and his apprenticeship commands, the war was over.

At Fort Dix, this author was subjected to constant pressure to sign up for OCS. Although, I don't know this for a fact, I suspect Steve Warner was subjected to similar pressure. At one point, my company commander, Captain James K. Ballard took me to see Lt. Col. Richard Ziegler, the executive officer of the 5th Battalion. Ziegler, a stocky former West Point football lineman, had once been a rising star in the Army. As a Captain in 1962-63, he had served as executive officer to the legendary Lt. Colonel John Paul Vann, then an advisor to a South Vietnamese Division in the Mekong Delta. Ziegler and Vann planned one of the most ambitious operations of the early Vietnam War, an attack on a Viet Cong unit near the village of Ap Bac in January 1963.

The halting and pathetic execution of Ziegler and Vann's plan by ARVN commanders allowed the vastly outnumbered Communist force to escape the battlefield after inflicting substantial casualties on the government troops, as well as killing several American helicopter crewmembers. The battle was important in confirming to American reporters Vann's assertions, that the optimistic assessments they were receiving from U.S. headquarters in Saigon, bore no resemblance to the truth. Ziegler's role and his photograph appear in one of the more popular Vietnam War books, *A Bright and Shinning Lie*, Neal Sheehan's biography of John Paul Vann.

By the summer of 1969, however, something had happened to Ziegler's career prospects. A rising star does not get assigned to be the executive officer of a basic training company. When pressuring this draftee to commit to OCS, Ziegler emphasized his belief that whatever one thought of the Vietnam War, a soldier should make the most of the situation in which he found himself. Opposition to the war, he said, was irrelevant to whether or not one should go to OCS and he indicated that he himself didn't think the war, or at least the way it was being waged, made much sense.

He opined that an intelligent, well-educated soldier would rue the day when he chose to serve out his time as an enlisted man, particularly, since he would have to spend much of his time with other enlisted men, for whom Ziegler indicated some degree of contempt. Although Ziegler did not accept no for an answer, he was placated by my commitment to seriously consider signing up for OCS.

Interaction with one's fellow enlisted men was somewhat of a shock to many college-educated soldiers. In the cubicle next to mine in basic training, none of the men had gotten past the tenth grade. I had, at some level, forgotten that there were Caucasians in the United States that never made it into, let alone through, high school. Three of the four soldiers in the adjoining cubicle were 17 or 18 years-old, white, from either Pennsylvania or New York, and had dropped out of school in the 7th or 8th grade. One of them, who had enlisted to be a cook, was notorious in the platoon for his obvious lack of personal hygiene. Once I lent him a clean white T-shirt, because he didn't have one to stand for inspection. A week later, he offered to return it after having worn it for an entire week. It was now almost black.

Curiously, during basic training, I found that I liked a number of the recent high school graduates and drop-outs better than many of the trainees who had been to college.

From Steve Warner's Vietnam notes and letters, I believe that he too found many of the less educated GIs more attractive than some of those whose backgrounds were more similar to his own.

Many of the recent high school graduates or drop-outs impressed me with their mechanical skills. Given my attitude towards the war, I was not particularly enamoured of some of those who had signed up for OCS and wanted to demonstrate how enthused they were with everything we were doing. Similarly, I became fond of many of the recently-returned combat veterans who were our cadre, particularly Sergeant First Class Edward E. Washington, a black career soldier, and Sgt. Dennis Cunningham, a wounded draftee serving out his term of enlistment. Like Steve Warner, I admired and even envied their courage in a war I despised.

On the other hand, there appeared to be a mutual antipathy between me and my platoon's college-educated drill Sergeant. Unlike most drill sergeants, he had never gone to Vietnam and had volunteered to attend drill sergeant school in exchange for a commitment that he would never leave Ft. Dix during his term of service. From the manner in which he ran our platoon, I concluded that, in college, my drill sergeant must have been the pledge trainer for a fraternity. In part, I felt, that unlike the combat-hardened cadre, my drill Sergeant had not earned the right to harass me.

For the college-educated draftee, the best way to keep one's options open was to wait and see what sort of assignment one received at the end of basic training. If you were going to be sent to advanced infantry training, you had nothing to lose by signing up for officer candidate school--particularly since it would delay your deployment to Vietnam for anywhere from 6 to 18 months. If however, you were made a clerk and survival was your primary objective, going to OCS made no sense at all.

The eight weeks of basic training in the summer of 1969 was more serious business than some of the trainees realized and despite the decreasing casualty rate, some of them would be killed in Vietnam between late 1969 and 1971. Besides Steve Warner, another who would die was 21 year-old Ross Bedient, from Valois, New York. Bedient, from basic company B-5-2, went to Vietnam as a helicopter mechanic in 1970. He died in a hospital in Japan from burns sustained three days earlier when his helicopter was shot down while transporting infantrymen in Tay Ninh Province.

Avoiding the Infantry

At the end of Basic Training, each soldier learned of his next assignment. On August 8, 1969, Steve Warner was assigned directly to the Public Information Office at Fort Campbell, Kentucky. This was rather unusual. Most soldiers were sent for advanced individual training for a specific military occupational specialty (MOS). If the soldier's primary interest was surviving military service, the training one wanted to avoid was MOS 11-Bravo, light weapons infantryman. While many other occupational specialties were dangerous, they were all less so. For example, a mortarman, 11-Charlie, generally did not get any closer to the enemy than the helicopter's landing zone.

Although this was very dangerous because the landing zones often came under enemy fire, the mortarman generally was not exposed to the dangers of being ambushed or setting off a mine.[74]

The 11-Bravo, often referred to as a "grunt," also lived a much more primitive life than even other combat soldiers. While helicopter crews, for example, could lead a very dangerous existence, they sometimes slept in a clean bed at a base camp. The "grunt" (a term derived by the sound an infantryman made when carrying around his heavy pack) often operated for weeks in the jungle, sleeping on the ground exposed to the elements-- without such creature comforts as bathing or changing clothes.

Conscientious Objection

On July 28, near the end of his eight-week training, Steve Warner wrote to the Central Committee for Conscientious Objectors. Mike Wittels of the Committee replied on August 11. Wittels first wrote that Steve was not necessarily disqualified from conscientious objector status by the fact that he would not refuse to kill in any conceivable war:

> The question is are you conscientiously opposed to war as you know it...I know a great number of men who started out thinking they were selective objectors, only to realize later that their objections--reached from the existential point of view-- were indeed to War.

Wittels recommended that, if Steve considered himself a selective objector, he apply for a transfer to noncombat training and status. Wittels did so because judicial decisions had made it clear that one was not entitled to conscientious objector status on the basis of opposition to a particular war, as opposed to war in general. Thus, if a young man conceded that he would have taken up arms against Hitler, he was legally obligated to submit to induction and go to Vietnam.

Wittels concluded his response by discussing the possibility of spending months in the Fort Dix stockade, citing the fate of the small number of men who had decided to refuse orders after they had been inducted into the armed forces. He suggested that it would be better for Steve to consider re-enlisting for another year, an option "that purportedly gives you the assignment of your choice."[75]

The definitive ruling on the issue of selective objection was rendered by the United States Supreme Court on March 8, 1971, three weeks after Steve Warner died in Vietnam. In *United States v. Gillette*[76] eight of the nine justices joined or concurred in

---

[74] Steve Warner noted, however, that an infantry company at times didn't take their mortars with them on a mission. When this happened, an 11-C was just another rifleman.

[75] The Army promised young men who enlisted for three years that they would be sent to advanced training in a program they selected. Thus, one could enlist to go to helicopter maintenance school. At least in 1969 and 1970, it is my impression that these choices were honored by the Army.

[76] 401 US 437; 91 S.Ct. 828 (1971).

the opinion of a Johnson appointee, Thurgood Marshall, formerly the NAACP's chief counsel. Only the quixotic William O. Douglas dissented.

Marshall's opinion rejected the contentions of Guy Gillette, who claimed entitlement to an exemption from the draft on the basis of humanistic religious objections to the Vietnam War. Gillette had been convicted of a willful failure to report for induction. He asserted that he was willing to fight in a war for the national defense or as part of a United Nations peacekeeping operation. He refused to serve in Vietnam, which he argued was an unjust war. The Supreme Court also rejected the appeal of Louis Negre, who was already in the Army and had received orders to go to Vietnam. Negre, a devout Catholic, contended that fighting in Vietnam violated his religious beliefs and had sought a discharge from the military.

The Court held that Gillette and Negre were not entitled to relief either under the Selective Service Act or the First Amendment to the United States Constitution. As to the latter, the justices held that neither the First Amendment clause prohibiting the establishment of religion nor the clause guaranteeing the free exercise of religion required Congress to recognize the objections of a draftee or a soldier to a particular war.

It should be easy to understand why the Court could not recognize selective conscientious objection after 50,000 U. S. soldiers had already died in Vietnam. First of all, a number of those already dead or maimed might have claimed such status, if they had thought they could have avoided Vietnam by doing so. On the other hand, it is not such a radical proposition that a nation that is supposedly ruled with the consent of the governed must have the consent of an individual when it sends him off to fight an enemy who clearly presented no immediate threat to the United States. The proposition is even less radical when the government clearly avoided, as in did in Vietnam and Korea, the Constitutional requirement that Congress declare war on the enemy.[77]

In a popular war, such as World War II, it takes an incredible amount of fortitude to reject induction on the grounds of opposition to the policy of the government. Those who claim conscientious objection will be subjected to tremendous pressure to conform to the social norm and accept induction.[78] Indeed, a government should, at least, in the short-term, be able to wage a popular war with volunteers. The Federal Government relied exclusively on volunteers for the first two years of the American Civil War. England also waged World War I for several years without resorting to conscription.

Only in an unpopular war would large numbers of young men, secure in the knowledge that they will not become social outcasts in their communities, avoid induction by claiming to be conscientious objectors to that war. Indeed, to do so suggests

---

[77] As the Persian Gulf War and 2003 Iraq War show, the Constitutional requirement for a congressional declaration of war is a dead letter.

[78] My father, who was 4-F during World War II due to a serious neurological problem, told me of his discomfort walking around in civilian clothes during the war when virtually everyone else his age was in uniform.

some sympathy or at least empathy for the enemy, which few Americans would be willing to express in the face of overwhelming support for military action--or cowardice.

Fort Campbell and Orders to Vietnam

Steve apparently made no more efforts to seek conscientious objector status. In August 1969, he completed basic training and was assigned to the public information office at Fort Campbell, Kentucky--40 miles north of Nashville. Virtually everyone else in his company departed for advanced individual training (AIT), a period of 8 weeks or longer depending on the MOS for which the soldier was being trained. Many draftees went for eight weeks training to become infantrymen, after which they received a short leave and were off to Vietnam. Although infantry AIT was conducted at several Army posts, the one with the most notoriety was Ft. Polk, Louisiana. Polk, which during much of the year had a climate similar to that of Vietnam, provided the infantryman with the best preparation for what was ahead. On the other hand, eight weeks at Ft. Polk was just another 8 weeks to be perfectly miserable.

Other soldiers went to an Army school to become cooks, radio operators or to be trained in other noncombat jobs. A few were sent to training at such posts as the Presidio near San Francisco, where they spent many months learning a foreign language. The few 2-year draftees sent to that program generally spent 9 months learning Vietnamese. Still others went to school to be tank crewmen, artillerymen, combat engineers, helicopter repairmen and medics. Each of the latter jobs could very dangerous in Vietnam, but still considerably safer than 11-Bravo.

While Steve was processing in at Ft. Campbell, a sergeant asked for volunteers for KP.[79] He promised that volunteers would not be assigned to KP again during in-processing and he kept his word. On KP that first day, Steve met and struck up a friendship with Dennis James, another soldier who had been drafted out of law school, who was assigned to the base's legal office. On January 13, 1970, Steve wrote Dr. Stemen, that "luck has been kind and I am now an Information Specialist. We're the guys that are supposed to make the truth fit to print."

Steve reported to Dr. Stemen that his chief activity had been researching and writing on subjects such as "elements of leadership" and the dangers of marijuana. Another piece he authored was entitled, "The high price of AWOL."[80]

At Fort Campbell, Steve also prepared a 15-page outline about the Peace negotiations taking place with the Vietnamese Communists in Paris. One of the officers in the Information Office planned to use the outline for an article on the subject. Steve

---

[79] KP, Kitchen Police, is one of the most onerous tasks in military service. KP involves a number of tasks and soldiers on KP have different assignments. The worst job is washing pots and pans; the best job is DRO (dining room orderly) which involves setting the tables and wiping them off after meals. For one assigned to KP, it was imperative to be the first one to the mess hall, so as to get the least onerous job. The last soldiers to report generally were assigned to pots and pans.

[80] Absent without leave.

was also proud of a two-hour lecture he rewrote for use in basic training on the subject of military heritage and achievement.

Steve told Dr. Stemen that he generally worked from 6:30 a.m. to 4:30 p.m. and had the rest of his time to himself. As a result, he was doing a lot of travelling--to such places as New Orleans, Memphis, Atlanta, Lexington, Paducah and the Great Smokey Mountains. Often he went with his fellow law school student/draftee Dennis James, who had a car. However, James insisted that they hitchhike to Memphis and, for the first time in his life, Steve went out to the road and stuck out his thumb. At Fort Campbell, Steve also developed a taste for country and western music. He and Dennis James drove to Nashville several times to go to the Grand Old Opery.

Steve, Dennis James and two other college-educated soldiers, Mike Touff and Jim Sturdivant, formed a close-knit circle of comradeship at Ft. Campbell. The four often traveled together, including a trip to Atlanta at New Year's and to Mardi Gras in New Orleans, just before Steve's departure from the Kentucky post.

Steve already had been informed that he would soon be receiving orders to go to Vietnam. When he received these orders, he had a long discussion with his friend Dennis James about whether he should go to Canada instead.[81] In his letter to Dr. Stemen, Steve said that, "I still find the Vietnam War a total disaster. Most of the Vietnam returnees I've talked to in the Army have no faith at all in the ARVN's (South Vietnamese Army) ability to make Vietnamization work."

Contempt for the South Vietnamese Army is a recurrent theme in the written and oral accounts of many American veterans of Vietnam--even those not obviously opposed to the war. Many soldiers wondered why the ARVN troops seemed to be inactive when they were fighting the NVA or Viet Cong. An example of this sentiment is this passage from *The Killing Zone*, a matter-of-fact war memoir by Lt. Frederick Downs, who lost an arm in Vietnam:

> We looked over our group of guerillas; there were eighteen. Soon a jeep and a deuce and a half drove down the road from the north, stopping next to the prisoners. A dozen Vietnamese soldiers jumped down, laughing with anticipation, arrogant as hell, kicking the Cong up into the back of the truck and pushing them around just for the hell of it. I didn't like them, the lazy bastards. Why weren't they out on patrol instead of us.[82]

---

[81] March 18, 2002 interview with Dennis James, Jr.
[82] Downs, Frederick, *The Killing Zone: My Life in the Vietnam War*, (1978) at page 193.

MAP OF SOUTH VIETNAM AND PHOTOGRAPHS

Photographs are Courtesy of the Stephen H. Warner Southeast Asia Photograph Collection, Special Collections, Musselman Library, Gettysburg College--unless otherwise indicated. They are identified with the Special Collections Department's image number.

The map of South Vietnam is from an Army Publication "Tour 365"--with notations showing places visited by Steve Warner

List of Photographs

Special Collections Image 1672: Stephen H. Warner

Steve Warner: College Yearbook Photo

Special Collections Image 1685: Photograph of PFC Michael Fillion conversing in French with a Cambodian schoolteacher. Steve Warner, with spiral notebook, is in the background.

Image 1715: PFC Michael Fillion. Photo by Henry C. Eickhoff, III, just prior to airlift back to Vietnam. Late June 1970

Image 1751: First Cavalry Division Troops in Cambodia, May or June 1970.

Image 1712: Shirtless troops with chaplain in the field. Steve Warner's superiors objected to their lack of proper military attire.

Image 1456: The "Fixer" crew, August 1970. L - R: SP4 Claire Nelson, crew chief; SP4 Harold C. Gay, medic; CW2 (warrant officer) Terence A. Handley (co-pilot); CW1 Robert Farrington (Aircraft Commander). On October 20, 1970, Handley and Gay were killed when their "dust-off" helicopter collided with an observation helicopter, while they were evacuating wounded infantrymen from the battlefield.

Image 1638: Medic Harold C. Gay (February 14, 1951- October 20, 1970) and the "jungle penetrator," used to extract the wounded from the battlefield.

Image 1651: Warrant Office Robert Farrington, the "Fixer's" commander. Note the USARV "dust-off" patch.

Image 1725: General William B. Rosson, Deputy Commander, Military Assistance Command Vietnam (MACV), inspecting an enemy cache captured in Cambodia in 1970.

Images 1541, 1542, 1543: Night Patrol of the 173rd Airborne Brigade fording a stream. Photos by Steve Warner late November-early December 1970.

Image 1554: Troops firing mortar. Note 173rd patch.

Images 1670-1671: 173rd Airborne Patrol in the bush--photos probably by Steve Warner.

Soldier from 173rd Airborne setting up a claymore mine.

Image 1458: Soldier named Munson, probably at FSB Green, Christmas 1970.

Images 2090, 13A, 14A & 15A: Co. A, 7th Engineers placing culverts in ravine with bulldozers and Armored Personnel Carriers during the first week of February 1971--photos probably by Steve Warner. Subject of Stephen Warner's last story.

Alfonso Varela's photograph of Co. A, 7th Engineers on patrol during Lam Son 719

Major Unit Locations
& PLACES VISITED BY STEVE WARNER

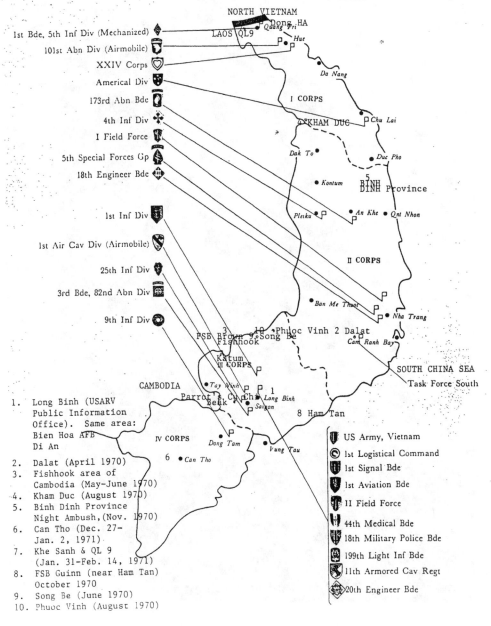

NORTH VIETNAM

1st Bde, 5th Inf Div (Mechanized)

101st Abn Div (Airmobile)

XXIV Corps

Americal Div

173rd Abn Bde

4th Inf Div

I Field Force

5th Special Forces Gp

18th Engineer Bde

1st Inf Div

1st Air Cav Div (Airmobile)

25th Inf Div

3rd Bde, 82nd Abn Div

9th Inf Div

Dong HA
LAOS QL9
Quang Tri
Hue

Da Nang

I CORPS

KHAM DUC
Chu Lai

Dak To
Duc Pho

Kontum
5
BINH Province

Pleiku
An Khe
Qni Nhon

II CORPS

Ban Me Thuot
Nha Trang

3
FSB Brown
Fishhook
10 Phuoc Vinh 2 Dalat
Song Be
Cam Ranh Bay

Katum
III CORPS

CAMBODIA
Tay Ninh
Cu Chi
1
Parrot's Beak
Long Binh
Saigon
8 Ham Tan

SOUTH CHINA SEA
Task Force South

IV CORPS
Dong Tam
Vung Tau

6 Can Tho

1. Long Binh (USARV
   Public Information
   Office). Same area:
   Bien Hoa AFB
   Di An

2. Dalat (April 1970)
3. Fishhook area of
   Cambodia (May-June 1970)
4. Kham Duc (August 1970)
5. Binh Dinh Province
   Night Ambush,(Nov. 1970)
6. Can Tho (Dec. 27-
   Jan. 2, 1971)
7. Khe Sanh & QL 9
   (Jan. 31-Feb. 14, 1971)
8. FSB Guinn (near Ham Tan)
   October 1970
9. Song Be (June 1970)
10. Phuoc Vinh (August 1970)

US Army, Vietnam

1st Logistical Command

1st Signal Bde

1st Aviation Bde

II Field Force

44th Medical Bde

18th Military Police Bde

199th Light Inf Bde

11th Armored Cav Regt

20th Engineer Bde

Special Collections Image 1672: Stephen H. Warner

STEPHEN H. WARNER, R.D. #1, Skillman, N.J. 08558, History Major, Pi Delta Epsilon (2,3,4), Phi Alpha Theta (3,4), *Gettysburgian* Feature Page Editor (2,3,4), Ad Hoc Committee of Students opposed to the Vietnam War (3,4), Alpha Phi Omega.

Steve Warner: College Yearbook Photo

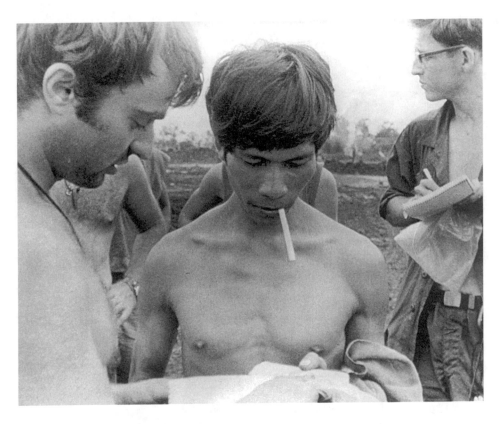

Special Collections Image 1685: Photograph of PFC Michael Fillion conversing in French with a Cambodian schoolteacher. Steve Warner, with spiral notebook, is in the background.

Image 1715: PFC Michael Fillion. Photo by Henry C. Eickhoff, III, just prior to airlift back to Vietnam. Late June 1970

Image 1751: First Cavalry Division Troops in Cambodia, May or June 1970.

Image 1712: Shirtless troops with chaplain in the field. Steve Warner's superiors objected to their lack of proper military attire.

Image 1456: The "Fixer" crew, August 1970. L - R: SP4 Claire Nelson, crew chief; SP4 Harold C. Gay, medic; CW2 (warrant officer) Terence A. Handley (co-pilot); CW1 Robert Farrington (Aircraft Commander). On October 20, 1970, Handley and Gay were killed when their "dust-off" helicopter collided with an observation helicopter, while they were evacuating wounded infantrymen from the battlefield.

Image 1638: Medic Harold C. Gay (February 14, 1951- October 20, 1970) and the "jungle penetrator,"
used to extract the wounded from the battlefield.

Image 1651: Warrant Officer Robert Farrington, the "Fixer's" commander. Note the USARV "dust-off" patch.

Image 1725: General William B. Rosson, Deputy Commander, Military Assistance Command Vietnam (MACV), inspecting an enemy cache captured in Cambodia in 1970.

Images 1542: Night Patrol of the 173rd Airborne Brigade fording a stream in Binh Dinh Province. Photo by Steve Warner late November-early December 1970.

Images 1541, 1542, 1543: Night Patrol of the 173rd Airborne Brigade fording a stream. Photos by Steve Warner late November-early December 1970.

"Night Fighters of the 173rd," Binh Dinh Province, November - December 1970

Image 1554: Troops firing mortar. Note 173rd patch.

Images 1670-1671: 173rd Airborne patrol in the bush--photos probably by Steve Warner.

Night Patrol of the 173rd Airborne in the bush: November - December 1970

Soldier from 173rd Airborne setting up a claymore mine.

Image 1458: Soldier named Munson, probably at FSB Green, Christmas 1970.

Images 2090, 13A, 14A &15A   Co. A, 7th Engineers placing culverts in ravine with bulldozers and Armored Personnel Carriers during the first week of February 1971--photos probably by Steve Warner. Subject of Stephen Warner's last story.

Company A, 7th Engineer Battalion moving a culvert into place during Lam Son 719, February 1971

Alfonso Varela's photograph of Company A, 7th Engineers on patrol during Lam Son 719

On January 31, 1970, Stephen Warner received orders to report to Fort Dix, New Jersey on March 16, 1970 for shipment to Vietnam. He "sat around Ft. Dix for a week" and boarded an airplane on March 21.[83] In the latter stages of the War, troops on the way to Vietnam flew on a commercial jet. Those planes chartered from passenger carriers, such as United Airlines, featured most of the amenities of a commercial flight, including in-flight movies. Those soldiers flying on planes chartered from freight carriers, such as Flying Tiger Lines or Overseas National, did not see the movies.

The flights either went due west across the Pacific, with stops in Hawaii and beyond, or via Alaska and Japan. One of the highpoints or lowpoints of the trip, depending on your status, was an encounter between troops coming home and those on their way to Vietnam.

Before he left, Steve dropped a note to his friend, Susan Walsky, telling her that, "I am now on my way to Nam to play my part in America's greatest military disaster." He assured her that "due to a very kind lady--called luck, I should come back whole in body and probably in mind." Thinking ahead, Steve closed his letter by telling Walsky that he planned to spend four or five months traveling around the world between the time he got out of the Army and his return to Yale.

After a flight of 24 hours or more, he arrived in Vietnam on March 23 (March 22 in the U.S. on the other side of the international dateline), or in Army parlance, "in-country." In his first letter home on March 24, he wrote:

> Things have worked out so perfectly that I'm afraid I'll wake up and it will all turn out to have been a dream. I arrived in country yesterday morning and like everyone else was hustled to Long Binh's 90th replacement battalion.

> Well, here are all these poor 11 Bravo [the Army's military occupational specialty designation for infantry rifleman] types being sent out to assignments with field combat divisions and I'm called for a personal interview at U.S. Army Vietnam (USARV) headquarters. Yup, the headquarters itself; three big 2-story air

---

[83] At about this time troops reporting for shipment to Vietnam often had to wait in the United States for a week or two, so that enough troops left Vietnam for the government to meet its April 1, 1970 troop ceiling. I reported to Ft. Lewis, Washington on March 26, and didn't leave for Vietnam until April 8--a two-week period. This was highly undesirable for a lower-ranked enlisted man for a variety of reasons. First of all, the clock did not begin to run on your tour in Vietnam until you boarded the airplane. The time spent waiting to be shipped overseas was in many cases "bad time"--in that it only prolonged the length of your service in the Army. Soldiers like Steve Warner or myself, who would have less than five months remaining in the Army upon return from Vietnam, would get out of the Army as soon as they returned to the States. Therefore, every day spent at the shipment post was another extra day in the Army.

Worse yet, a soldier in transient status was subject to being put on KP or undesirable work details on a constant and haphazard basis. Unlike a GI assigned to a unit, there was generally no duty roster to spread the misery around in an equitable fashion. I pulled KP twice during my 2-week stay at Fort Lewis, 2/7 of my KP experience in the U.S. Army.

conditioned buildings with flush toilets and electric water fountains.—add lots of generals and other assorted brass—all on top of a hill.

…I'm deposited in this large room full of desks and suddenly kids start coming. It turns out [there are] ½ a dozen [Fort] Campbell garrison company graduates at USARV headquarters—"garrison looks after its own."[84]

I was "hired" by the Sergeant Major though no one really knows what I'll be doing. I think eventually I'll be writing command information topics for USARV. All the kids who work on the hill…live in a common group of barracks – "hootches." Even here we have flush toilets –very rare critters in NAM! We also have a very nice little bar with a TV and refrigerators with cold beer in the center of our hootch. …the interiors of the hootch [are] broken down essentially [into] semi-private rooms—all very nice. We even have 2 mama sans (Vietnamese women) who, for $10 a month, do all your laundry, keep your boots shined and act as maids in cleaning up your room and making your bed![85]

As far as my personal safety is concerned, don't sweat it. Long Binh base hasn't been attacked in over two years by ground forces. As far as the rockets—well, they've never come close to USARV headquarters, where I'll work, or my barracks—SO RELAX!…I've been warned that the press often writes up rocket incidents on Long Binh base as if USARV headquarters itself was hit. What they mean is no more than that a rocket hit somewhere on base—a rather large place with a 45-mile perimeter and 30,000 troops! In order to hit me in my office, the rocket would also have to blow up one 3-star general and assorted lesser stars! So again relax.

On March 30, Steve wrote Dr. Stemen about his assignment. He noted that Army would be doing a background check on him. He observed that he was sure that the Army investigators would be very interested in his activities with the Ad Hoc Committee against the War in Vietnam. Steve commented to Dr. Stemen that the U.S. State Department had just announced that it had lifted its prohibition against U.S. citizens travelling to Communist China. Steve said that he would be very interested in visiting Red China when he got out of the Army.

On April 5, Steve made notes[86] on his conversations with several enlisted men that were responsible for the assignment of incoming enlisted personnel to units in Vietnam. He noted that one from Fort Campbell had:

---

[84] This is Steve's parody on the often-repeated semi-official slogan "The Army takes care of its own."

[85] The "mama sans" at least in Long Binh and in Saigon were older, rural women—there was no suggestion that they were available for sexual favors. The amenities of garrison life in Vietnam was an unexpected and very pleasant surprise to enlisted men coming from posts in the states, accustomed to doing all menial tasks for themselves. Better yet, "KP" duty, i.e., washing the dishes and pots and pans in the mess halls in Vietnam was performed by Vietnamese civilians, not the enlisted U.S. Army personnel.

[86] 27 spiral notebooks in Steve's handwriting are in his papers in the Special Collections Department of the Gettysburg College Library, in addition to a number of smaller notepads. Although, his handwriting left a lot to be desired, he was an excellent freehand sketch artist. For example, in his notebooks, there are a

Taken care of all the Campbell kids who have come in since and visited him. Campbell now has 3 enlisted men in assignments at headquarters and 2 in the Information Office (IO) at headquarters. Also, he put people in crucial spots throughout Nam and has beautiful contacts...here was a kid who essentially assigned thousands to die. Probably the most powerful EM draftee in Nam.[87]

Steve was assigned to the Public Information Section of the USARV headquarters information office. On April 3, 1970, he described his new job to his parents:

PI is definitely the place to be. Our primary job is to get out a daily press sheet on what happened in the war during the last 24 hours. All night long various units from all over Nam phone into our office with reports. Two PI guys take down the reports, rewrite them and the next day after being ok'd and checked by several different layers, they are taken to Saigon and distributed at the "five o'clock follies," the US Army's daily briefing for the press.

You may wonder what the rest of the PI staff do since there are 4 officers and about 8 enlisted men, and as I indicated it really takes only 3 guys to put out the daily press rag. Well, the rest of us don't have much to do at all, in fact, keeping from going crazy with boredom is the biggest job. To keep from going crazy we run all around Nam writing stories on anything we think of...We propose stories, get the ideas ok'd and then are free to take off anywhere...for up to a couple of weeks...The stories are then distributed to various periodicals and papers.

The set up is really incredible. I've been issued a pass, which is good for anywhere in Vietnam. We get second priority for hopping on all aircraft...I get one day a week off and Saigon, off limits to most GIs, is only one hour away by military bus. [My] press card entitles me to all the accoutrements that a Major is entitled to. These include the right to use the officer's club [and] sleep in officers' barracks. (The guys say actually it's much more interesting to stick with the enlisted men)...most important of all, it entitles us to typewriters and jeeps with drivers when we want them...

---

number of very good sketches of soldiers sitting across from him on an airplane. Deciphering his notebooks is more difficult than it otherwise would be because on some occasions he started writing from opposite ends of the same notebook.

[87] Few enlisted men arriving in Vietnam got the opportunity to personally visit the enlisted assignment office. The office obviously had some screening mechanism, which allowed it to pick out highly educated or skilled arrivals. This author was sent to the same office as Steve Warner about three weeks later. I had been introduced to the commanding officer of the U.S. Army Procurement Agency Vietnam at the Pentagon and he had requested that I be assigned to his command. However, the staff at Long Binh did not seem to be aware of his request until I asked them about it. Then they asked me if that's where I wanted to go; I said yes and was on my way to the Procurement Agency in Saigon the next day.

> I must admit I'm slightly horrified at being a writer – I've had no experience. But I guess I'll pick it up and what an opportunity to really see what's going on and practice writing. The IO [information office] crew is an incredibly diverse bunch. Photographers, writers and audio men basically. One guy was with a Madison Avenue agency...before he was drafted. Another fellow majored in international relations at Georgetown...he'd just been hired by the New York Post the week before he was drafted—almost all are draftees and all are marvelously cynical.

In the margin of this letter, Steve Warner suggested that his parents save his letters and mentioned his plan to document his experiences in Vietnam and provide the material to the Gettysburg College Library. He then returned to the subject of his personal safety:

> THE BIG THING IS FOR YOU FOLKS TO RELAX. USARV IO, since its creation about 4 years ago has only lost one man and that guy died of malaria after he returned to the states. He hadn't been taking his malaria pills! I take mine with none of the aftereffects, which are so famous.
>
> I gather from the guys who go out that the field troops take mighty good care of us...like everyone they are pleased at the thought that reporters have actually come out to write about them and maybe even their names [will appear] in the newspaper back home.
>
> Though our press reports indicate a dramatic increase in Charles V[iet] Cong's escapades the last several days, except for a bit of distant bombing, the only evidence at [Long Binh] was three nights ago—the first night Charlie [the Viet Cong] renewed activities. ...about 7:30, 5 Cobra helicopter gunships went rushing over our hootches as we sat drinking beer and watching a movie...

On April 6, Steve informed his parents of his decision to travel around South Vietnam, again playing down the danger to which he might be exposed:

> ...[USARV] headquarters is located at Long Binh, 17 miles north of Saigon on a former rubber plantation...Uncle Sam chopped down all— and I do mean every last one of the trees—so Long Binh is quite bare.
>
> The Major asked me if I wanted to travel and I said absolutely yes, so I'll be bopping around. Don't worry—in its four years IO USARV headquarters has lost only one man...the generals' housing complex (17 generals live there) is only 800 feet from our barracks, so you can see we're in good company. Charlie...isn't interested in hitting enlisted

mens' barracks, he much prefers to hit equipment (it's harder to replace!)…Also, he's an excellent shot with his rockets so he doesn't normally hit hootches by accident either.

…I wrote Dennis James, the Georgetown Law fellow I bummed around with at [Ft.] Campbell, who is coming over in May, to send me a copy of his orders and I would see if I could get him assigned here. Well, the orders came today …so I'll see what I can do.

I had to take some stuff to Di An…today. Di An is where the 1st Infantry Division is headquartered.[88] They are going home next week to the states, at least officially. In reality, 340 will return with the flags, about 6000 will leave within the next 60 days and over 8000 poor souls will simply be transferred to different units in Nam.

…the trip was cool. My first chance to see rural Nam (I've been down to MACV in Saigon twice).[89] Peasants working in rice paddies, water buffalo, temples, women cranking water buckets from wells—the whole works.

Steve's parents sent him a letter in mid April in which they expressed an interest in hearing about the places he had visited. After remarking upon the fact that their letter took only 5 days to get to him from New Jersey, he replied on April 20:

I'm glad you want to hear about my wanderings…frankly I couldn't decide whether or not it would be best to keep totally silent…so you wouldn't worry about me wandering all about or tell you (in mildly censored versions) about my trips since they are definitely what will make my year….describing them is the best way to assure you I'm not just mowping about.

He then told his parents about an interview he conducted with a soldier, SP4 Alex Gibson of Charlotte, North Carolina, who in the States had built engines for a number of famous stock car drivers. This was one of the first human-interest pieces Steve wrote for distribution in the United States. He described how difficult it was to conduct this interview, since, "I know absolutely zilch about stock car racing." At the time of the interview, Gibson was a transportation inspector, giving final approval to vehicles that had been brought in for maintenance. Based on his interview, Steve wrote a press release entitled, "He Keeps Them Running." Steve also discussed a trip he and bunkmate

---

[88] Located only a few miles from Long Binh.

[89] MACV, the Military Assistance Command Vietnam, was the overall headquarters for American military activity in Vietnam. Located at the Tan Son Nhut Air Force Base on the outskirts of Saigon, it was home to the senior commander of U.S. forces, i.e.,—William Westmoreland (throughout the years of the heaviest fighting) and Creighton Abrams (Westmoreland's successor and commanding general during 1970-71). MACV provided assistance to the South Vietnamese Army (the ARVN) as well as direction to the American army, navy, marine and air force commands.

Sherman Carlson took to Saigon. They visited the Saigon zoo and were surprised to stumble across the Vietnamese National Art Museum, "full of ancient Vietnamese art."

Shortly thereafter he traveled to Dalat in Vietnam's central highlands, a city favored by the French colonial administration as a resort due to its elevation and cool climate. There he studied the Army's procurement of vegetables from Vietnamese vendors and wrote an article about it.

In his notebook, Steve observed:

> Charlie doesn't bother the veg[table] operation supposedly because he is collecting a toll on the produce coming into Dalat.

He also wrote:

> They shipped 600 U.S. rangers in here during Tet…and after Tet removed them and replaced them with 500 Viet rangers. Feeling among several EM [enlisted men] at dinner (no dissenters) was that Charlie could take Dalat any time he wanted.

Finally, Steve noted that Dalat was a "delightful hill resort"… very European in feeling."[90]

Steve's observations about the precarious security of Dalat were confirmed soon thereafter when the Viet Cong temporarily overran the city. The two officers Steve met with while covering the vegetable operation, Captain Earl Manning and Lt. James Larson, were shortly thereafter brought back to Saigon, where this author worked with them at the headquarters of the Army Procurement Agency. My own letter home of July 10, 1970 recounts my conversation with Larson about his hair-raising experiences in Dalat:

> Today I was talking to a Lieutenant who was in the Agency's office in Dalat, which just closed. He said it could really be a fantastic resort (it is pretty high up and cool) but there are at least 3 VC battalions operating right outside the city. Last month the VC overran Dalat for three days. None of the hundred or so Americans (no combat troops) were hurt. However, he said his wife was worried sick for a day and a half--because the radio in the U.S. said Dalat had been taken by the VC and it didn't say anything about US casualties (zero) for about 36 hours. Anyhow, even with the hot and humid weather, I gather he is very glad to be in Saigon.

---

[90] Gettysburg Collection, Notebook 7, notes of April 27, 1970.

While at Dalat, Steve became very ill and was hospitalized at Nha Trang with a temperature of 103.6. While he was there approximately 20,000 American soldiers invaded border areas of Cambodia for the first time during the war to confront Communist troops. South Vietnamese soldiers had preceded the Americans into Cambodia. Two areas of Cambodia bordering on South Vietnam, called "the Fishhook" and the "Parrot's Beak" due to their physical configuration, had been major staging areas and supply depots for Viet Cong and North Vietnamese forces operating in the central and southern areas of South Vietnam.

President Nixon announced the invasion on April 30, 1970. He predicted that the operation would last from between six to eight weeks. The primary objective, he told the American people, was not to kill enemy soldiers but to destroy their supplies and drive them from their Cambodian sanctuaries. Nixon justified the incursion as necessary to protect the lives of American troops in Vietnam and to shorten the war.[91]

Opponents of the War viewed the invasion as a major escalation of the war by the Nixon administration and an indication that the President had no plans to withdraw American forces from South Vietnam in the near future. Anti-War demonstrations erupted all over the United States--particularly on college campuses.

On May 4, 1970, at Kent State University, near Cleveland, Ohio, National Guard soldiers opened fired on demonstrators, killing four. However, Kent State became synonymous with the anti-war demonstrations only after the killings. Tension over the administration's continuation of the war had been building at colleges and universities all over the country throughout the late winter and early spring. At normally conservative Miami University in Oxford, Ohio students engaged in a "flush-in" in April which depleted the town of Oxford's water supply. When this author left the school three years earlier, the anti-war movement was small and regarded by most students as a lunatic fringe.

On April 30, *The New York Times* reported battles between crowds of students and police at Ohio State University in Columbus. Seven people were shot. The May 1, edition of *The Times* carried a front-page photograph of Ohio National Guardsmen confronting students with fixed bayonets on the OSU campus.[92]

After the Kent State shootings, the nationwide demonstrations increased in their intensity. For example, 2,800 students battled 250 policemen on the Madison campus of the University of Wisconsin. Police used tear gas to disperse demonstrators at the University of Texas in Austin. Student "strikes" also came in vogue. A number of

---

[91] *The New York Times*, May 1, 1970, 1:1.

[92] Ohio Governor James A. Rhodes sent 1500 National Guardsmen to OSU as well as sending guardsmen to Kent State.

schools, including Boston University, closed for the rest of the school year. At Harvard Law School 700 students voted to strike for remainder of the term.[93]

The day before Kent State (May 4 in Vietnam, May 3 in the U.S.), Steve wrote two notes, one expressing his general bitterness and the other focused on his frustration over events in Cambodia.

> ...Coming to Nam destroyed my whole idealistic personal philosophy. I shall make Nam pay by forcing her to stuff me so full of reality's many fruits that none shall dare call me an idealist, untouched by life's unpleasant aspects. And if I die, it shall have been worth it...

Although Steve immediately asked his boss, Cpt. Edward Cashman,[94] for permission to join the American soldiers in Cambodia, he heartily disapproved of the invasion. In another note written on May 4, he said:

> ...according to the press the only offered reason [for the invasion] is to stop a possible communist attack for 4 or 5 months. Nothing more....No doubt the Communists will now feel they have to overthrow the Cambodian government and put Sihanouk[95] back in and what do we do when S[ihanouk is] back in power...and what do we do when he gives the Communists unlimited use of Cambodian ports....

> ...what's a liberal to do. Those of us in the Army can get perhaps a little personal comfort from our impotency being traditional. But what about the people back home...they seem to be as totally impotent as we are....

> How I despise that little imaginary man called Mr. Silent Majority.[96]

---

[93] *The New York Times,* May 6, 1970.

[94] As of this writing, Cashman is a judge in Vermont.

[95] Prince Norodom Sihanouk headed the Cambodian Government until March 1970, when he was overthrown in a coup led by his prime minister, General Lon Nol. Ethnic violence raged in Cambodia, with Cambodians murdering members of the Vietnamese minority. Communist Cambodian and Vietnamese troops battled the Cambodian army. On April 14, 1970, Lon Nol appealed for foreign [i.e., American] assistance.

In April 1975, two weeks before the fall of Saigon, the Cambodian Communists, the Khmer Rouge, captured the capital of Phnom Penh. Upon seizing power, the Khmer Rouge, forced the country's urban residents into the hinterlands. There the Khmer Rouge waged a genocidal campaign against their own people, murdering over a million individuals between 1975 and 1979. Defenders of the President Nixon's Vietnam policy point to the atrocities committed by the Khmer Rouge as evidence that he was right. Opponents argue that the Khmer Rouge would never have come to power but for the Lon Nol coup, which they argue was at least tacitly encouraged by the United States. Moreover, they point out that it was the North Vietnamese Army, albeit for its own interests, that stopped the genocide when it invaded Cambodia in 1978 and 1979.

[96] President Nixon repeatedly claimed that, while a vocal minority opposed his continued prosecution of the Vietnam War, a "Silent Majority" supported him. The results of the 1972 Presidential election would seem to bear him out on this point. Richard Nixon gave the majority of Americans what they wanted. After Tet,

What a horrible, sterile small-minded petty ass he must be.

Steve compared those who supported President Nixon to the crowds of Germans who cheered Hitler at Nuremberg and the Italians who supported Mussolini.

After two months, American troops withdrew from Cambodia. Henry Kissinger, Nixon's national security adviser, claims that the invasion virtually ended the war in the southern half of South Vietnam until well into 1972.[97] He made no claims as to any more permanent benefits. Stanley Karnow's assessment is that the invasion relieved the Communist military pressure on the Saigon area. However, he concludes that:

> ...the triumph was temporary and, in long-range terms, illusory. The Communists were soon able to supplement their lost equipment from the vast stocks furnished by the Soviet Union and China.[98]

On May 6, Steve wrote to a law school friend, Isadora Wecksler, about his plans to write a book about his year in Vietnam upon his return:

> I image it will be a sort of Berlin Diary [William Shirer's account of covering the news from Berlin just before and just after the outbreak of World War II] approach but much shorter. On the one hand—a first person narrative of what a headquarters IO man saw and heard in a year of travelling and reporting in Nam and on the other the feelings to the year's events of an individual actively against the war in college and one who seriously thought about refusing to come...anyway, it gives me a goal to push for, a reason to always ask that final question and spark up that final conversation and sit down and put it...on paper.

Steve asked about the reaction on the Yale campus to the invasion of Cambodia and the killing of four anti-war demonstrators at Kent State by Ohio National Guard troops. These events, he said, "made him sick. I want to cry but that will have to wait. Right now there are experiences to gain, facts to learn." He also wrote his parents the same day:

> We in IO—the enlisted men, are totally and literally sick at the mess in Cambodia, not to mention the problems back home of which the Kent State massacre is the most blatant example. When will America wake up that this war is tearing out our very soul. [It is] raising bitterness and hate which can't help but linger long after the killing has stopped and only the maimed in body and mind remain.

---

the majority of the public desired two mutually exclusive things. It wanted the war to end and at the same time did not want the United States to capitulate to the Communists.

[97] Henry Kissinger, *The White House Years*, p. 987.

[98] Stanley Karnow, *Vietnam: A History*, p. 625. The invasion horrified a substantial number of draftees, such as this author, who were stationed in such rear echelon areas such as Saigon, Long Binh and Bien Hoa. Ironically, it may have significantly enhanced our personal security.

My God, Nixon and all the nice proper spokesmen for the silent majority scream out against the violence on the campus and protests and yet what choice do they leave us. What noble models of devious deceit and violence they present.

Steve ridiculed the President's justification for the Cambodian invasion, i.e., that it would thwart an imminent Communist offensive in the Saigon area and disrupt enemy support activities for five or six months:

> ...all this is suppose to magically end in two months and things [will] settle down as if nothing happened[?]...what stupid asses we have in Washington and what stupid asses that are willing to stand for it all in the belief that this bit of escalation—unlike every other one of the war—will 1) be temporary and 2) actually shorten the war.

> ...what about Mr. Nixon's speech last week calling the college protesters bums as compared to those fine young men in Nam. Mind you, you only have to go to college and protest—which means disagree in public with Mr. Nixon to be a bum and only have to be in Nam to be a fine young man.

> ...everyone smiled when we "went clean for Gene." It was so cute....But something went wrong when the kids didn't silently fade away after June but instead went to Chicago to try to get things done....[99]

> ...something is wrong when the President announces a 150,000 troop cut and that Vietnamization is going great with the kind of victory we want within our grasp, and ten days later finds it necessary to invade a neutral nation for the safety of our own South Vietnamese forces...but we have to trust him. After all he has more information than we do.

BELIEVE ME THE HATRED AND BITTERNESS THAT WILL BE THE HARVEST ARE IMMENSE.

On May 9, the Information Office's record of never having lost a man in combat came to an end. Although Steve apparently never mentioned this to his parents, he was greatly affected by the death of his friend Wiley Hooks. Nevertheless, he was undeterred in his determination to travel in the field in order to make his year in Vietnam a personally satisfying experience:

---

[99] Steve is referring to the campaign activities of a number of anti-war students on behalf of Senator Eugene McCarthy, who challenged President Johnson for the Democratic nomination in 1968 due to Johnson's prosecution of the Vietnam War. Many of these students cut their hair and modified their dress so as to not alienate adult voters. He also refers to the activities of anti-war activists who went to Chicago to protest the war at the time of the Democratic National Convention at which Vice-President Hubert Humphrey was nominated for President. A full scale riot ensued involving the students and the Chicago police department.

Death came to HQ USARV-IO this afternoon. I took the afternoon press run to Saigon and came back to be greeted by the news that Wiley Hooks was killed this morning about 10:30 when his helicopter went down in Cambodia.

Strange, when it comes so close. Wiley is the first death ever in this office. Supposedly, he was in a Cobra [an assault helicopter], which would make it more ironic. When we were in Nha Trang two weeks ago, I talked to him about riding in a Cobra...he said it was a bummer because of [lack of space]. You can't even go out on a real mission. Well, it sounds like he finally got to go on a real mission.

He liked to go where the action is. When we were in Nha Trang, he was trying, scheming, plotting to get up to do some tapes of the kids...What more is there to say...he was fun, always ready with a bit of wit, a fellow who knew his job and did it well. [He was] restless, much happier out travelling than being here at Long Binh. He kept telling me on the Nha Trang trip that the stories weren't at the main bases but back in the boonies....

[I have] no added feeling of bitterness or hate of the war—nothing that grand—just the realization that the next round of casualty figures will include a friend—someone with a name, a face, a personality—a real flesh and blood human, I knew.[100]

In writing his parents two days later, Steve did not mention the death of his friend. Rather, he emphasized what he regarded as the opportunities presented by his situation:

Ignoring my original objections to coming over here (which I think are still valid but all history now), I wouldn't give up what I'm doing now for the world. I'm seeing so much, learning so much and experiencing so much that it's like 4 years of college (a very liberal arts college) condensed into a single year. It's going to make me a vastly better writer, and interviewer—both valuable traits back in the world—and give me just much more understanding of what makes people...tick. I have a crazy knack for finding the best in most situations and enjoying it in my own peculiar way....

Steve asked his parents to send him more 6-inch by 3 ½ inch spiral notebooks, which he said came in very handy in conducting interviews with field soldiers. He noted that they were small enough so that he could keep one is his shirt pocket at all times and that they allowed him to take notes without intimidating his subject.

He also noted that when he went to Saigon, the products of his father's company, Johnson and Johnson, were much in evidence on the Saigon black market. "Next to

---

[100] Gettysburg College Collection, Box 1, Notes in folder.

Seagrams and Eastman Kodak, Johnson and Johnson is one of the real movers on the black market."[101]

Steve traveled back and forth between Long Binh and Cambodia by helicopter. He wrote in his notebook on May 14:

> Here I sit in FSB My[ron]....I'm filthy, I stink and the great red blotches of sun burn on my arm bode bad for tomorrow...But I am happy, exhilarated. This is where it is at....[102]

On May 16, Steve wrote a memo to his immediate supervisor, Cpt. Edward Cashman,[103] requesting permission to go to Cambodia on a long-term assignment:

> Sir, Cambodia is where it is at least until 30 June and it [will be] a crime if we don't have our whole [office] (at least that portion of it [that] wants to go) out there every moment we can...other stories can wait, Cambodia will not wait...there is history being written out there by the gobs and I want to record it....
>
> As for personal risk well, I came in as a draftee and Lady Luck didn't make me a grunt though she could have. If she wants to turn nasty now or at a future date, she can get me anywhere in Nam and I'd prefer it be where I'm really accomplishing something...Cambodia until 30 June.

Cashman approved Steve's request with a note, "be careful and keep your head down." In preparation for his assignment Steve attended a four-day orientation for combat troops from the 1st Air Cavalry Division. He had to jump off a 35-foot high tower and rappel down on a rope. He noted that it took him six tries to jump.

At the training site, Steve got a second chance to throw a live grenade:

> I confess I don't think I've been so scared in my whole life as throwing the grenade. They wouldn't let me throw one in Dix. Said I was too lousy a shot.
>
> Well, I threw it, not very far, but no one got killed or hurt.[104]

---

[101] On the first things that struck this author upon his arrival in Saigon was the great inventory of luxury goods available for sale on the street. I thought this odd for a nation supposedly fighting for its very existence. The next thing that struck me was that none of the Vietnamese seemed to be doing anything productive. The women were all serving the U.S. military as secretaries, mama sans or bar girls, depending on their level of education. The civilian males either worked for the Americans or in the economy servicing the Americans, i.e. as laborers, clerks, barbers, cab drivers and mess hall workers.

[102] Gettysburg Collection, Notebook 8, notes of May 14, 1970.

[103] Cashman, an attorney, was receiving legal periodicals from his wife. Steve told his parents he would try to look at them because "it would be nice if I knew a wee bit of law when I return to Eli's (Yale's) hallowed halls."

[104] Gettysburg Collection, Notebook 23, entry of May 16, 1970.

Steve also attended a lecture on the Geneva Convention and the laws of war. This lecture was a thinly disguised attack on the soldiers who revealed the My Lai massacre to the American press. He noted that:

> Implicit throughout the lecture is the E6's [the staff sergeant presenting this portion of the orientation] inability to understand why people go back to the world [the United States in the parlance of the US troops in Vietnam] and tell of crimes and get others in trouble.

> The E6 said, "gentlemen, when someone goes back to the world and shoots his mouth off, you can be in a world of hurt from one little incident."

One of the instructors told Steve about a B52 attack against an enemy hospital complex in Cambodia the previous year. This sergeant said he had been in an infantry unit that had been helicoptered into Cambodia to attack the site, but they were driven off with significant casualties. The B52s then came from Guam and leveled the complex. Afterwards, the instructor's unit returned. As Steve noted, if the story was true, the mission had to have been conducted illegally with the knowledge of some very high-ranking brass.[105]

From what he learned at the Cavalry Division orientation, Steve concluded:

> This war as evolved by the U.S. is based on helicopters and fire support bases covering all NAM. The Viets [ARVN] don't and won't have the copters we have or the trained personnel and equipment for the FS bases. Yet, these are the twin pillars of the allied effort. What happens when the Viets we've trained in this type of strategy try it without the copters and the artillery?[106]

Steve also got some practical advice from a more experienced PIO specialist, Mark Jury. Jury told him to: never walk behind the rear blade of a helicopter; never stand in front of an artillery piece—otherwise you're likely to have your eardrums blown out; and to roll down your sleeves onboard a helicopter—to increase your chances for survival if the copter crashed and burned.

As he prepared to return to Cambodia, Steve agonized over what to tell his parents:

> Really can't make up my mind on what to tell Mom and Dad on Cambodia. I guess it will depend on the reaction to my tirade letter. I've got to tell them someday about Cambodia because I presume they will get

---

[105] The bombing of neutral Cambodia, which began in March 1969 and continued for 14 months, was not officially acknowledged by the United States until 1973.

[106] Notebook 23, entry of May 19.

wind of my articles. The point is to get across that I'm doing it because I really want to and enjoy it immensely.[107]

The Public Information Office published Steve's story "The Hats At Headquarters" in its Press Release of May 17, 1970. The article was researched in mid-April[108] and written prior to his first departure for Cambodia. In a somewhat veiled manner, the story tackles Steve's growing uneasiness with the contrast between the plight of the field soldier with his own enviable situation.

> Hats make a difference in the Republic of Vietnam. The man who places a steel helmet, or not, on his head every morning and then spends the day sloshing through rice paddies with an M-16 rifle at the ready experiences a very different Army from the olive drab baseball-capped GI who spends his days in equally important, but considerably less glamorous, support activities at a base camp.
>
> The pot and the cap normally go their separate ways. The infantry soldier, a "grunt" in the vernacular of the war, may spend a few days in base camp resting between missions but he can be no more than a blur to the busy clerks and other support personnel. In turn the support soldier may don his steel pot and M-16 to pull perimeter guard but that is normally no more than another detail, relatively safe except for the always possible activities of a skillful explosives-carrying enemy sapper.
>
> Occasionally the members of these strangely alien, but equally vital, worlds receive the opportunity to experience the other's mode of life. One such place is the Security Detachment assigned to Headquarters, United States Army in Vietnam (USARV) at Long Binh, 17 miles northeast of Saigon.
>
> Here approximately eighty combat-hardened men chosen by their field units as deserving a reward for past valor and wounds are charged with guarding the USARV headquarters complex.
>
> For the men assigned to the Detachment the shift from the world of combat to the world of the garrison soldier is shockingly sudden. The Security Detachment's personnel requirements are relayed down to the field battalions who select the men from among the outstanding individuals in the field--the men who deserve a break.
>
> The news can come with shattering swiftness to the individual soldier. One young sergeant was in the midst of an extensive field operation when a radio message came over ordering that a landing zone be cleared and he immediately be flown to battalion headquarters. When told of his new

---

[107] Notebook 23, May 19, 1970.
[108] Gettysburg Collection, Notebook 7, notes of April 14, 1970.

assignment the confused sergeant, not realizing what it entailed, frantically tried to be switched back to his old assignment until someone took him aside and explained the new job.

But the shock of changing worlds has only begun. Whisked out of the ironic security of a small close knit unit and the friendly informality of the field, the new guard finds himself plopped in the midst of the United States' largest military installation in South East Asia, a base with more generals, headquarters and GIs than most field troops ever imagined could be gathered in one spot.

After a quick processing in and a brief refresher on the do's and don'ts of military courtesy, the new man discovers himself in the strange world of the garrison soldier. "It's weird at first," remarked Specialist Four Jerry Doddridge, a six-month infantry veteran with the 1st Infantry Division, from Cambridge City, Indiana. "You're used to being sloppy and the first thing they do is pour you into starched fatigues and spit polished boots and set you marching and saluting." But these changes are cheerfully accepted by the men who realize that along with the new benefits of showers and clean uniforms each day come the responsibilities associated with representing all the "grunts" at this--the Army's Vietnam headquarters.

With the guard sites situated well within Long Binh's perimeter there is little danger normally from "Charlie." Instead the guard shifts are consumed in a vital but routine series of checking authorizations to be within the area, spot checking out-going vehicles, and most of all just being at the designated spot, ready, should anything go wrong. Twenty-four hours a day, 7 days a week, the guard continues, with the length of time the men are off between shifts fluctuating with the unit's strength. "It's a pretty difficult job for men used to the excitement and variety of the field," points out Captain Darrel Powell, a native of Kinta, Oklahoma. Sometimes a new man will actually come to the Captain and request reassignment to the field, fed up with the routine quality of his new job. The Captain, as does approximately 75% of the Detachment's personnel, wears at least one Purple Heart.

Gradually the guards adjust to garrison life. However, habits acquired in the field die slowly. Almost every guard can cite at least one incident in the first few weeks at Long Binh when field acquired reflexes placed him in a ridiculous situation. For one pair it was low crawling down to a bunker to realize only upon arrival that a truck had merely backfired. Along with the field reflexes come the crudities of field acquired language and manners. Some members of the Detachment surprise themselves at how fast these battlefield relics disappear. All are very happy to have a chance to polish up before confronting wives, mothers and sweethearts.

What does the return from the field mean to these men? For Specialist
Four Dale McCoy, wounded four times while in the field and a native of
Anderson, Tennessee, the joys include "...a cold shower, to be able to sit
at a club, a bunk and most of all no tensed up feeling all the time."
Specialist Four Patrick Victor, who spent 7 1/2 months in the field with
the 199th Light Infantry Brigade and comes from Staten Island, New
York, put in somewhat differently, "When you're in the field you don't
have a past, a future or a home. You're out there cursing to yourself. Here
you know you're probably going to make it home. You can begin to make
plans again."

Of course there were good times in the field as well as bad and even the
best adjusted guard sometimes finds a chopper whirling overhead or the
orange streaks of tracers from some distant fire fight carrying him back to
the field. Time after time a guard would try to explain the intense pleasure
which taking a shower offers after going without for 25 days, or what it is
like to set down the M-16 for a few minutes in the field and play some
football or a few hands of hearts. But most of all the guards dwelt upon
the closeness that grew between them and their buddies in the field. With
the free time and varied recreation opportunities at Long Binh each man
rapidly goes his individual way with something gained but something also
lost.

Nowhere is the attitude of the men of the pots more dramatically
expressed than in the evening lowering of the colors at retreat. To the men
of the Security Detachment, who daily raise and lower the flags of the
republics of their homeland and Vietnam at USARV Headquarters, the
ceremony has personal meaning. As one guard said, "It feels good to
lower those flags, they represent a lot of our friends."

On about May 21, Steve visited "Rock Island East" the largest North Vietnamese
supply base found by American troops (so named in honor of the U.S. Army supply
facility at Rock Island, Illinois). He also visited Fire Support Base Brown, which had
been subjected to a ground assault by Communist forces a week earlier. He wrote to his
parents on May 28:

What was groovy was that while we were there, they decided to abandon
the base and so everyone hopped into a super convoy of trucks, tanks,
jeeps, etc. and bopped through the Cambodian jungle for two hours to the
new base. It was a blast, after one stopped being depressed by all the
devastated villages and the downed chopper and the bridge the NVA had
blown up the night before.

The natives are really groovy. Very primitive...PLEASE TRY NOT TO
WORRY. Believe me I'm having a ball.

***

The Cambodian thing does not appear to be going well. We've got quite reliable rumors that there may be a US thrust into Laos or [towards] Phnom Penh [the capital of Cambodia] in the near future.

Finally Steve mentioned that the monsoon rains had begun. FSB Brown was hit by an 18-hour downpour, which flooded the GI's underground hootches to a depth of between 5 and 10 feet. The flooding knocked out communications for a while and the storm made helicopter support for the base impossible.

On June 8, Steve returned from an extended stay in Cambodia, including 7 days at Fire Support Base (FSB) Neil. In a letter home, he commented bitterly about the Army flying a congressional delegation out to Snoopy's hill, two miles from the base:

> It's such a stinking farce to troop them over to show off the cache site after you've talked to the kids who took the hill. Roughly 121 of them started up and they made it to the top 7 days later with 61. 50% casualties for one stinking cache, which could have probably been bombed to smithereens—but of course then there wouldn't have been anything to show off. To be fair, I have to admit there is evidence that no one knew a cache existed...but I have a pretty good suspicion that the brass thought the hill was full of junk.

Steve then mentioned to his parents that he was thinking of hitchhiking from India to Europe when he got out of the Army. Also for the first time, he mentioned a recurring dream—to go to New Guinea, buy a large quantity of primitive art and resell it in the United States. His friend, Dennis James, recalls that Steve often had ideas of how they could make money. On several occasions he told James that they should invest in companies that produced microwave ovens. Steve believed that in the future more and more people would be living in mobile homes and that they all would need microwaves to cook.

After telling his parents about his plans to make money reselling primitive art, Steve returned to his experiences at FSB Neil:

> The next night it was raining and we forgot to put out the claymores [mines] which combined with the fact that the concertina wire at the point was all broken down (everyone was using it as a shortcut to get to the choppers' landing zone)—meant we had a marvelous hole through the firebase's defenses. Fortunately, Charlie decided not to come in.

***

One afternoon we were sitting around and bemoaning the lack of ice, beer and sodas. Suddenly, someone suggested that I catch a chopper (since I can come and go as I want), fly back to Vietnam, buy the stuff and bring it back....I enlisted the aid of another fellow to help me carry the junk and at 3 p.m. we grabbed a chopper for Song Be. We got there about 3:30, I borrowed a fellow's ration card that I know at IO there [and] rushed down and bought 6 more boxes of cigarettes for trading, while the other fellow bought 6 cases of beer and coke. Then we stole some ice and rushed over to the chopper pad where by a super miracle, we found a chopper going back to Neil. At 5 p.m. we were back at Neil on the very front line sipping beer and cokes with real honest to goodness ice.

The chopper truly sets the tone of this whole war. Time wise the front and rear are seldom more than 15 or 20 minutes apart, even in Cambodia.

Steve closed this letter by marking the places he'd been on a map. He noted that he'd spent one day riding with helicopter assault missions into Cambodia. "Lots of fun and not nearly as dangerous as it sounds."

On the contrary, the troops that Steve was visiting were not so sure about their safety at FSB Neil. Steve observed in his notebook entry of May 31:

...the fellows are spooked to a certain degree. Keep coming up against rumors that there is a regiment or couple of companies [of NVA] right in the area.

They mention the huge mortar that was found in the cache and think if the NVA had it. Again there are rumors the NVA have artillery and the guys...could speculate what tanks could do to the FSB.[109]

During July, Steve wrote a piece entitled "The Hootch That Jamie Built",[110] which some of his peers considered his best article. It included an account on his escapade to Song Be, albeit leaving himself out of the story.

Without explosives Jamie could not have built his house.

In fact, Jamie's "hootch" was built of explosives--twenty Bangalor torpedo crates which if full would have been enough to blow a good portion of the fire support base out of Cambodia and back into Vietnam.

Jamie began his hootch upon arrival at the 1st Cavalry Division (Airmobile) base. Here he would remain until his foot completely healed and the doctor approved his return to the field.

---

[109] Notebook 18.
[110] The Gettysburg College collection contains Steve's drafts of July 15 and 16, 1970; not the final version of the article.

After three days the engineers reclaimed their Bangalors and down came the hootch. It was obvious that the hootch must be rebuilt. This time Jamie built [it with] empty 105mm howitzer ammunition boxes.

Inside he gave the May [Playboy] centerfold the place of honor opposite the door. Around her hung a guardian host of shapely creatures who grew more beguiling with each passing day.

At some point--nobody knows exactly when--Jamie's hootch became a home. The unrecorded event probably took place one evening, for evenings were when the hootch came alive.

Jamie assured the event when he made the oil lamp from an old Pepsi can with a wick fashioned from a machine gun bandoleer. The flickering light of the burning kerosene magically lured those passing by into Jamie's home, until six, seven or even eight men were talking and playing cards, but mainly talking within the hootch's crowded walls.

The lantern drew the soldiers, but Jamie C. Thompson, III, held them. Drafted at 25 after a leisurely seven years of college, the former resident of Barrington, Illinois, found himself within a year, an infantry sergeant in Vietnam.

Jamie enjoyed people and people enjoyed Jamie.

One night a young infantry soldier, straight in from the field, dropped by and talked of the recent death of a buddy. "It ain't no fun to see your best buddy killed beside you. All you can do is be thankful it's not you, and sometimes you almost wish it was."

Jamie and the others offered a few sympathetic words and more importantly an understanding ear as slowly, ever so slowly, the poisoning memory worked its way out.

Sometimes, within the hootch, there was a bit of talk about politics--the pros and cons of the war, the meaning of Kent State. Mostly, however, the words were more personal--talk of "the world", that far off place whence Jamie and his friends came and where they hoped to return.

A young soldier, struggling manfully to grow a mustache, mentions his problems in writing letters home which don't tell all the truth but will ring true to his wife and parents. Two others discuss the future joys of the new Cougars this hellish year's earnings will purchase. Still others quietly speak of marriage and future plans for school.

All this is small talk but dreadfully important when the enemy lies just outside the base in a strange and often terrifying jungle.

But Jamie's home is not a melancholy place. Men enmeshed in danger cannot afford to be melancholy.

The card games are famous and a new one always welcomed.

One night the group found a Montagnard ax with a strange curved handle. The men passed it from hand to hand, each recipient thinking up and acting out a new imaginary use for the old tool, a pipe, a cane, a shovel, a pool cue--how about a snorkel tube, on and on the ax passed for over an hour.

If lady luck felt munificent[111] there were cokes and beer and even a bit of ice at night. Sometimes these would come through proper channels, but more often they arrived by one of those ingenious means fighting men invent.

The strangest of these was the great Song Be raid. Bewailing the lack of beverages and ice one afternoon, a chopper suddenly inspired Jamie and the band to action.

Why not catch the next bird back to Nam, buy the needed supplies and then grab a chopper back to the base? Of course, there could be difficulties if caught, or if no chopper returned that evening, but in [a] crisis such as this, risks must be taken.

A raiding party of two was dispatched and soon they were back in Song Be, 20 miles away and on the other side of the border. Six cases of beer and soda were quickly purchased but the ice presented more difficulties. None could be found.

In the midst of loading the cases onto a conveniently sited chopper, the two raiders spotted a trailer filled with ice. As the chopper revved up, the mad raid continued with the shouts of a furious sergeant following the pair. As they jumped back into the chopper, ice in hand, an obliging pilot immediately took off.

That night the crowd was thick and the smiles wider in Jamie's hootch.

Jamie went back to the field but the hootch remained. It had taken on a life of its own from the flow of GIs who passed through its doors.

---

[111] very generous.

That is why no one was really surprised at the first thing the hootch's new occupants did. They rebuilt the hootch that Jamie built, bigger and better than ever.

Steve's June 15 letter home dealt less with his experiences and more with his anger over the war and the invasion of Cambodia in particular:

> The news gets more gloriously worse by the hour. The night that Cambodia essentially ceded half of herself to the NVA, a couple of us here had a modest celebration of sorts. Really quite funny, [I] figure the fall of Phnom Pehn should about coincide with Nixon's big victory celebration after the withdrawal of all US troops on the 30th. The war is lost, every man who dies, dies uselessly.
>
> A brief interruption from these treasonous thoughts—the Bird (Full Colonel)[112] dashes in to tell me a bit more [about] all the glorious stuff he hopes I can get.
>
> …I really don't believe [that] anything less than incredibly horrible defeats (hopefully costly in land and materials only) is going to drive home to the folks in the US that this Viet mess has gone too far and we must write it off.

***

> WE HAVE LOST THE WAR IN SOUTHEAST ASIA. ANY FRANTIC STEPS TO COVER THIS UP ARE ONLY GOING TO MAKE THIS MESS BIGGER.
>
> …If the weapons and rice are in fact being replaced nearly as fast as we take it, no lives are in fact being saved. The only change is instead of the NVA being primarily in the border region they now occupy Cambodia.

Steve went back to Cambodia from June 17 through June 30. He returned to FSB Neil where soldiers from A Company of the 5th battalion, 7th Cavalry (5/7) Regiment, lst Cavalry Division and a few combat engineers with bulldozers destroyed all traces of the firebase. Then the troops spent four days gathering trash and burning it and then bulldozing the site. Steve accompanied Company A as it was helicoptered off of FSB Neil to a bomb crater on a hill six kilometers from the Vietnamese border. It then took them six days to walk back to a base camp in Vietnam. Steve described the terrain as very hilly and covered by dense bamboo. The troops avoided trails and stayed on high ground to avoid being ambushed by the North Vietnamese. Much of time, the troops

---

[112] Col. Alfred J. Mock, who arrived in Vietnam in mid-May 1970 to take command of the Public Information Office.

were crawling on their knees, but happily they encountered no NVA or VC. Before they left FSB Neil, on or about June 21, the soldiers had an encounter with Montagnards living near the base that gave Steve the material for the following press release issued by USARV in July:

THANK YOU

by

Specialist Four Steve Warner

LONG BINH, VIETNAM (USARV-IO)—"Thank you" can make a difference in the jungles of Southeast Asia as well as on Main Street, U.S.A.

If Bun Loeung, the Cambodian school teacher, hadn't said thank you, the American soldier[113]happily handing out cigarettes to the loin clothed Montagnard men and their colorfully dressed women would have walked right by.

But Bun Leoung did say thank you in his clear and almost Britishly precise English and soon he and the soldier[114] were deep in conversation. Such was the opening encounter between Bun Leong, the school teacher, and the men of the 1st Cavalry Division (Airmobile) station at Fire Support Base Neil, deep in the Cambodian jungle.

Several days later Bun Leong's thank you proved its worth when a delegation from his refugee village announced that the villagers wished to return to Vietnam with the departing American troops. They were terrified that the North Vietnamese soldiers would kill them once the Americans left.

Bun Leoung was called in[115] to act as translator between the baffled young Army captain and the excited Montagnard delegation. But poor Bun Leong's English was just not up to the occasion. It totally collapsed under the complexities of trying to arrange to move 800 people across a national boundary and assure them protection from the North Vietnamese on the way.

In the midst of the crisis someone[116]remembered that Bun Leong spoke French. To everyone's surprise an interpreter was soon conjured up from the infantry company's own ranks. Out stepped Private First Class Mike Fillion, Ludlow, Massachusetts, an infantry platoon radio operator during the company's

---

[113] Steve wrote "me" in the copy of the press release sent to his parents.
[114] "me" also inserted.
[115] "I suggested" is written in on Steve's parents' copy.
[116] "me" again inserted in writing.

81

almost two months in the Cambodian jungle but now, momentarily, an international interpreter. Back in Ludlow, Mike just happened to have gone for nine years to a parochial school where French was mandatory beginning in kindergarten.

At Mike's first words of French Bun Leong's face lit up with a huge grin and the negotiations renewed with a new vigor. The battalion intelligence officer just stood by looking puzzled and helpless. Slowly he shook his head and muttered. "Amazing, out here in the middle of the Cambodian jungle an infantryman and a native speaking French to each other."

Sometimes there were minor crises as when Mike frantically thumbed through his worn little French-English dictionary moaning, "they didn't teach me how to say shoot and explode in French class." In the end however, all the business was successfully completed and it was agreed that while the Montagnards would have to walk to Vietnam the U.S. Army would provide an air or ground escort.

As the negotiations broke up Mike held out the tattered dictionary and said "here, this is for you." Bun Leong smiled and thanked him.

The negotiations turned out to be for nothing for that night at a meeting in the refugee village, as Bun Leong put it, the "big man" decided that no one would go to Vietnam and all would return to "same, same" hamlets they'd abandoned to flee to Neil's protection.

But there was more to come. The very last morning of the American presence in this bit of Cambodia, as the only remaining company was gathering to be helicoptered out, a scout reported North Vietnamese soldiers in the area. He'd been told by Bun Leong's fellow villagers who had even drawn a map.

Some of the soldiers couldn't understand why the Montagnards had told the scout. After all the Cav was leaving and the NVA returning.

But one fellow knew the answer. As he said, "underneath their different styles of dress and colored skin people aren't much different the world over. If you treat them with dignity and respect they'll treat you right." The speaker wore the dirty, faded jungle fatigues of an infantry soldier long in the field and his skin was black.

On July 2, Steve wrote his parents about his desire to emulate Ernie Pyle, the journalist who became extremely popular in the United States during World War II writing about the individual soldier:

I've located someone to use approximately as a model of the kind of stuff I want to turn out, Ernie Pyle of WW II fame. All personal stuff on the little soldier—the forgotten man. The little soldier is a groove to talk to and often quite enlightening.

***

What sold me on Ernie Pyle was the bit on the inside of a book by him. It said "he hated wars, but loved the men who have to fight them." That about sums me up too.

Steve asked his parents to find and send him copies of some of Pyle's newspaper columns, since all he had was the journalist's autobiography. Finally, he told them that on his last day in the jungle, he and his photographer had taken 42 pictures of individual combat soldiers, which he called "hometowners". He took down each soldier's home address and planned to send an 8 x 10 photo to each of their homes as well as to their local newspaper. He found the troops to be "incredibly appreciative." He wrote the following piece to be sent with the photographs to the local newspapers:

LOCAL SOLDIER BACK IN GOOD OL' NAM

by
SP4 Steve Warner

NOTE: See attached personalized insert sheet for data to place in story's insert blanks.

LONG BINH, VIETNAM (USARV-IO) –(Insert #1), a resident of (insert #4) is back in good ol' Nam.

(insert #3) is a (insert #5) with Alpha Company, 5th Battalion, 7th Regiment, First Cavalry Division (Airmobile). The infantry company was helicoptered into Cambodia on a combat assault on May 6th and immediately set to work building Fire Support Base Brown, named for its captain. Three days later, the fire support base completed, Alpha moved on.

Fortunately they built well for on the night after Alpha left Brown its new residents were subject to the heaviest ground attack launched against any U.S. fire support base during the entire Cambodian operation. Fifty enemy soldiers lost their lives in the futile attempt, compared to only four U.S. wounded.

Alpha Company spent most of May and June tramping through the dense Cambodian jungle in an area thick with enemy caches.

Late in May after a heavy engagement the troops captured a major enemy medical cache. A careless North Vietnamese soldier kindly lent the troopers a helping hand. He had carefully sketched a map of the cache area on the top of a wooden crate and then abandoned it. The map, found by Alpha Company, clearly identified the six hiding places of the medical supplies which the enemy had scattered over an area of several acres.

During the second week in June, after another heavy engagement, the men took an elaborate bunker complex complete with 150 tons of neatly sacked rice.

The troopers put the rice to good use. Instead of digging their nightly fortifications in the hard, root filled clay, they built them above ground out of the solid bags of rice. Said one soldier, "rice stops bullets as well as dirt, and it's a lot less trouble." Before the men left the area they loaded the rice onto helicopters and it was flown back to Vietnam.

From the rice cache the men of Alpha returned to their battalion's fire support base, FSB Neil. Four days later the base was vacated by all but Alpha which spent the next few days in a giant clean up campaign, burning or burying all vestiges of Neil's existence.

But Alpha still had one final mission in Cambodia.

On June 24th the Company combat assaulted to within 4 miles of the Vietnamese border. The next five days the men spent inching their way through incredibly dense bamboo forests and over hills so steep that at one point the men actually cut steps in a hill to assist in climbing its steep slope. Much of the time was also spent checking out possible enemy cache sites previously spotted from the air.

Finally on June 29th at 10AM the unit crossed a tiny stream at the bottom of a densely foliated gorge. Alpha Company and (insert #2) was back in good ol' Nam.

The next day (insert #3) and his fellow troopers flew to Bien Hoa, the 1st Cavalry's rear, for three days of well earned rest.

As one Bien Hoa soldier said to a tired Alpha trooper, "Welcome back, you certainly deserve a rest, and thanks for making life back here a lot safer."

At the bottom of the first page of the copy of this press release, that Steve sent home, he wrote, "My proudest thing—because the guys will get individual credit!!"

In an entry in his notebook dated June 30, Steve noted a change in his attitude towards being in Vietnam:

Vietnam is rapidly ceasing to be places and events for me and instead becoming faces and individuals. How utterly wonderful. If I can continue in this direction all year I may yet have something worth publishing.

Strange but it looks as though my most meaningful protest against the war will be becoming totally immersed, wallowing in it so I can tell it through the men themselves...If they can do it for a year, I can do it for long enough to at least glimpse what their year is like from the inside. I really am happiest when I have an ideal that I'm guided by.

On July 4, Steve provided his parents with a more detailed account of his experiences:

Our combat assault out was cool. First, came the cobras [helicopters], 4 or 5 in a great spread out circle just sweeping around and around over our little hill. Then one by one they began to make trial passes over our little clearing in the bamboo....

After the cobras had done this a bit, they began to come over again and fire rockets of some sort into the ridge across from us...I was quite appalled at such power going off so close. I can't imagine what it is like when a company calls in artillery next to its position or gun ships. After this we had a mad minute. Everyone lined up either on the crater facing the ridge across the ravine or on the opposite edge of the crater into the bamboo. At a signal from Cpt. Walsh[117] (after he repeatedly told the guys "aim low, only at the hill directly across from you, we don't want to shoot down any choppers"), the crater exploded into a roar of rat tat, tat and M-16s [rifles], I think M-60s [machine guns] and one 45 [pistol] went off. I refrained and observed all. Number one, my weapon was so dirty, I wouldn't have been surprised if out of shear spite it would have blown up in my hands...Number 2, I just don't like the silly things, not just the 45s but all of them....

...Anyway, next came in this chopper which went around and around our little hill spewing out a super smoke screen....Well, as the smoker spun about his duty, the 6 pick-up birds glided over the horizon in single file. It really is a grand sight. All this marvelous blue sky and great puffy monsoon clouds and these 6 little birds bobbing along, one after another in what...the grunts call a duck walk. To me it looked more like 6 minnows or tadpoles swimming along in single file.

Suddenly, the lead bird would fly off the line and sweep down over the bamboo with a great roar of wind, dust ...the door gunners would lean far out and stare intently down at the ground, giving the pilot guidance through the intercom, the bird would slowly come down and settle itself amidst the bamboo stumps and grass....

Steve went on to describe how when the helicopters came in to pick up the troops, the pilot landed only one of its skids on the ground because of the slope of the terrain. Five soldiers who had been given a number corresponding to that helicopter's flight then

---

[117] Cpt. John Peter Walsh, Jr., West Point Class of 1968, according to Steve's notes, became company commander on June 9.

ran towards the helicopter and jumped aboard with all their equipment. Each helicopter made three trips between FSB Neil and a fire support base 4 kilometers away. Steve boarded helicopter number 17.

After returning to Vietnam, the entire 5th battalion was given three days rest at Bien Hoa, the huge post and Air Force Base adjacent to Long Binh. The soldiers of company A invited Steve to join them but he had to turn in his time-sensitive material and returned to his office at Long Binh. He then washed, shaved and changed his clothes for the first time in ten days. Steve returned to his hootch just in time for a steak and beer blast which lasted from 7 p.m. to 3 a.m.—however, he was so exhausted that he went to bed at 9. He observed:

> The incredible contrast of this…at such close juxtaposition makes you want to scream and cry. The inequity of it all….But, of course, if the fellows in our hootch were in the field and the fellows in the field were in our hootch, the parties would be just the same….

Some of the soldiers from the 5th battalion came to visit Steve at Long Binh and he accompanied them to the Loon Phoon Chinese restaurant on the post. About 100 of the 5th battalion men were at the restaurant that night. Steve accompanied them back to Bien Hoa and expressed his anger at the fact that busses were not provided and that these field troops had to ride in the back of open trucks in the rain during their brief respite from combat. He noted that the next morning the 5th battalion soldiers were awakened at 4:30 a.m. and sent out to an unknown destination in the field.

As a postscript to his July 4, letter, Steve returned to the subject of Ernie Pyle. It had occurred to him that his desire to emulate Pyle, might be disturbing to his parents, since Pyle was killed by hostile fire in the Pacific in the closing days of World War II:

> P.S. I trust I didn't horrify anyone by talking about Ernie Pyle [in my] last letter. One thing I plan definitely not to imitate about the gentlemen is [that] I plan to walk away from my war correspondent experience—alive.

> Oh yes, I've decided if I had it to do all over again, I'd come to Nam as a limited CO and be field medic. Not perfect for all my objections but quite workable and now I wouldn't be scared too! I wouldn't have to carry a weapon!!

After his parents sent him some material on Ernie Pyle, Steve wrote back on July 24, that what he really wanted was copies of some of Pyle's World War II columns:

> What I'm after is his style and technique for writing an individual column which takes diverse incidents and gives unity to them, etc. What I want to see is how in the hell he works his material. I'm sure I've got potentially nearly as great material (if I can just develop the eyes, ears and heart to find it) as he had from WW II. I just have to learn how to mould and polish it.

> ***

> I'm having a superb time fighting the censors (reviewers at MACV)...Well I got stuck this month doing the damn daily battle wrap up for the press. It means number one, I can't go anywhere at all except Saigon, and number 2, my hours are 4 AM (but I never come in until 5) to [noon].

> ...MACV has lots of rules as to what we can and cannot put in the battle wrap up. Many of these rules I find very stupid and worse they make the wrap up into a distorted piece of inaccurate propaganda rather than the wrap up on US Army action in the last 24 hours, it is supposed to be.

> So I've been sticking stuff in which we haven't in the past stuck in, but which I thought should be included. Mainly [these are] some rather grim little incidents up in the top of the country where US units have got the sh__ knocked out them.

> So three days ago this Marine Major who is a reviewer down there calls me up on the phone and royally chews me out for including this stuff. He says if we don't straighten up he is going to tear the damn thing up, etc. etc. and gave me directions as to what not to include. He also tells me that

anytime a US unit has been seriously mauled we don't list the number of casualties but rather call them light (I'm not kidding, this is official MACV policy) unless the unit has been hit so hard it no longer can function and then the casualties are moderate....

Well I mentioned it to my Captain (Cpt. Edward Cashman), who mentions it to my full bird Colonel (Col. Alfred Mock), who calls the Major's full bird Colonel, who chews out the Major! Our bird even came down and personally apologized to me, which I thought [was] quite nice.

The next day I follow the Major's and MACV's stupid rules. The result is [that] our release told only of 2 US troops as being wounded and makes no mention of 3 engagements where 6 GIs were killed, 5 wounded and 4 missing (these incidentally are high casualties for right now).

Steve closed this letter by mentioning that he was thinking about writing a book about his experiences in Vietnam upon his return. He also wrote that while he'd been working on the night shift at Long Binh, a number of soldiers from the 5th battalion, 7th Cavalry Regiment had dropped in to visit him on three different occasions, and one of them accompanied Steve on an outing to Saigon.

July 31, 1970 was Steve's last day on the night shift at Long Binh. He submitted a travel itinerary for August which was approved. His first trip was to Song Be near Cambodia to visit a Montagnard refugee village. A Roman Catholic nun had started a program in the village to produce handicrafts for commercial sale. Steve mused that, "perhaps, I can even pick up a bit of good stuff...."

His plans then called for him to spend three weeks in I Corps, the northernmost of the four military sectors of South Vietnam, which extended from the so-called "demilitarized zone" (DMZ) at the North Vietnamese border to below Da Nang. He rejoiced in the fact that he had "no one to report to. Just travel and see what I can find. [I] have lots of groovy ideas." He asked his parents to send him tape eraser for his typewriter.

Steve also hoped to spend a few days in Hue, the second largest city in South Vietnam and the scene in 1968 of some of the most brutal fighting of the War. Unlike most of his past trips, Steve was not accompanied by a photographer. He noted that:

I guess I'll be shooting most of my own stuff. The quality of photos no doubt will suffer, but being one man I should be able to better melt into the units I visit. That's one of the great virtues of travelling alone—you are forced to be more outgoing.

He complained about the MACV censors to his parents again on the 31st, and expressed great pride in his profiles of individual combat soldiers:

...we are trying another [tactic]. Just keep downgrading the battle wrap up until it can finally be buried. We killed the early night shift yesterday and my shift is going to begin to come in at 6:30 a.m. instead of 5 a.m.

Big deal of the week is I got my Alpha Company hometowners mailed out. Really, I'm much prouder of these than even of my best stories. Not that the Alpha Company story is very good, it's only fair to middling, but to the kids involved and their families, etc., it is a million times better than the best features.

I'll enclose a set of what I sent to each paper. One individualized set [is going] to the hometown paper of each of the guys. I also sent a copy of the story and the personal photo to the guys' parents or wife or girl – whoever he listed...until further notice.... I'll just set out to do some good individual hometowner stories on that grubby little forgotten creature, the field trooper. They appreciate it, it makes me feel good and makes big statistics for the Army, so everyone is happy. (The FEATURE stuff I'll write when I get time or just store my notebooks until I get home).

Steve had some problems getting some of his individual photographs cleared in his office.

Alpha Company's men were not at their prettiest when I shot the photos. Many had been wearing the same clothes for two months and hadn't really washed in nearly as long. Their hair was long, they were unshaved, etc.

Well, our # 2 man in IO [the Public Information Office] was shown the set proudly by my Captain. LTC X,[118] that is the goon's name, looked and muttered. He looked some more and muttered some more. Finally, he announced firmly that 'our soldiers in Vietnam, don't dress this poorly.' Captain explained that they'd been in the field for two months and that the shots had been taken as they were waiting a pick up. LTC X answered, 'I don't care, our soldiers just don't dress this poorly.' Well, he nearly killed the whole bunch, he wanted [to] but the Colonel [Mock] backed us.

Steve did not have very many opportunities to write home during his travels during August. He did, however, write about his trip to the Montagnard village near Song Be, where he spent two days, and wrote a story about it entitled "Treasure in Phuoc Vinh." His story was allotted two thirds of a page in the Army newspaper, *Stars and Stripes* and was picked up by other publications as well.[119] He and his photographer bought $110 worth of native handicrafts.

---

[118] Author's note: I have deleted this officer's name because I believe it serves no legitimate purpose to include it.

[119] November 2, 1970 letter to Susan Walsky. A number of Army publications picked up stories written by the USARV PIO. These included the *Stars and Stripes,* as well as the magazines, *Armour* and *Army Digest.*

Even when he didn't write home, Steve kept somewhat of a diary in his spiral notebooks, in addition to using them when interviewing others. On August 2, 1970, he wrote:

> [It] feels good to be off again...for the GI in Vietnam the key is to make time go fast not make the war end fast.
>
> No one thinks in terms of accomplishing things to end the war but rather in terms of staying alive for the one year the war is his war.[120]

The next day Steve analyzed his role in the war:

> ...the roughest part of being a reporter and trying to cover the field for me is my own embarrassment at having the audacity to come to "look at them." To be an observer by profession when you know they must live and die, it's hell. To have the gall to ask a grunt to tell you about his experiences so you can write them down.

Bravery in his position, Steve noted, wasn't confronting physical danger:

> Because you share it, it is quite endurable, it's the bravery of going into the midst of a group of men--you and they both know you are different-- and living down their stare of envy, snarls of contempt and guilt.

Finally, Steve confessed that there was a danger of trying to pretend he was a grunt and being a complete phony.[121]

On August 10, he informed his parents of his plan to spend a week on leave in Japan in September. Soldiers in Vietnam, at least those in the rear, generally took one 7-day leave and one 7-day R & R trip during their one-year tour of duty. Most married soldiers flew to Hawaii for R & R, where they met their wives, who had been flown in from the States at government expense. Unmarried soldiers tended to favor the other designated R & R spots, particularly Sydney, Australia. However, many also went to Hong Kong, Taipei and Bangkok.[122]

Soldiers on leave did not have the same priority for travel as did soldiers on R & R. They generally had to find their own way out of Vietnam and either had to fly standby on a military flight or pay for their trip out of their own pockets. On leave, GIs could go to locations that were not officially sanctioned and sponsored R & R sites, such as Japan. Steve planned to stay away from Tokyo and spent his week in Kyoto and Nara.

---

[120] Notebook 15.

[121] Notebook 15.

[122] The R & R centers in Taiwan and Thailand, and possibly elsewhere, steered GIs to specific bars at which the proprietors introduced them to prostitutes to keep them company during their stay.

In a letter home dated September 1, Steve noted that since he had not written for a while he would provide his parents with a summary of his recent activities. However, first, he asked them to speak to a Mr. Hogan, who had been his troop leader in the Boy Scouts to obtain the name of the manufacturer of the Boy Scout mirrors. Steve wrote that the mirrors available at the PX were worthless in the field because they were glass and easily broke in a rucksack. The scout mirrors were metallic and small enough (2" x 3") to fit comfortably in a soldier's pack. Steve planned to order a couple of hundred Boy Scout mirrors, which he thought would cost him about $25 and distribute them to combat soldiers as gifts.

He described his travels in August as beginning with a flight from Tan Son Nhut Air Force Base on the outskirts of Saigon to Da Nang, where he attended an official briefing. Steve then flew further north to Phu Bai and then to Camp Eagle, headquarters of the 101st Airborne Division. He had planned to spend several weeks at Camp Eagle but found a lack of enthusiasm for his mission, so he flew to Chu Lai, the headquarters of the Americal Division. From Chu Lai, Steve flew to Kham Duc, a small outpost about 40 miles west of Chu Lai and only eight miles from the Laotian border.

Kham Duc had been the site of U.S. Special Forces (Green Berets) camp until it was overrun by the North Vietnamese in 1968. In July 1970, soldiers from the second battalion of the first regiment (2/1) Americal Division returned to Kham Duc, to guard the small airstrip, which was being used to support ARVN operations in the area. When Steve arrived, the soldiers of the battalion had been constantly patrolling the jungle and steep mountains that surrounded the airstrip. Every two months, the troops were given a three-day rest period; four days if their company was selected as the most outstanding of the battalion. Steve described Kham Duc in a note to his hootchmate Sherman Carlson:

> Kham Duc is a gas. It is the site of a great Green Beret fiasco in '68. Surrounded by mountains and ravines on all sides. The joint consists of an airstrip and little green beany [beret] fort.[123]

Steve noted that it was rumored that Kham Duc might be the jumping off point for an ARVN strike into Laos, or on the other hand that it might be subject to a major North Vietnamese attack.[124] On August 18, Steve noted that "rumors are that we are to be hit the 19th" and that rumors had an NVA regiment heading for Kham Duc; "Who knows?"[125]

Steve took 63 individual photographs of GIs at Kham Duc to send to their hometown newspapers. He also spent a lot of time investigating potential human-interest stories that he could write about. He also made friends to the extent that he considered Bravo (B) Company of the 2nd Battalion, 1st Infantry Regiment of Americal to be one of

---

[123] Notebook 22, entry of August 15, 1970.
[124] Notebook 22, entry of August 12, 1970.
[125] Notebook 27, entry of August 18, 1970.

his two favorite companies in Vietnam. The other being A Co 5/7 1st Cavalry. Steve noted that he was depressed to leave Kham Duc after "a superb seven days." A major reason for his sadness was his expectation that some of the soldiers he had befriended would almost certainly be killed or maimed before the end of their Vietnam tour.[126]

Steve also conducted a lengthy interview with a platoon leader in B Company, Lt. John C. Shoemaker, a University of Massachusetts graduate from Brockton, Massachusetts. Shoemaker had been in Vietnam since April 1970 and told Steve that he volunteered for Officer Candidate School (OCS) because he was within a few weeks of being drafted. Shoemaker was married and had a child he had not yet seen.

They had a long conversation about marijuana use among the troops. Shoemaker told Steve he would turn in any soldier he caught using marijuana because he would get in trouble if he did not do so. On the other hand, the Lieutenant opined that a soldier would have to be pretty stupid to get caught by him because he certainly wasn't going out of his way looking for marijuana users.

Shoemaker also told Steve that he had disciplined two soldiers who refused to walk point [lead a patrol] and that three members of his platoon had been killed while he had been in command. One of them was shot in the head while walking right in front of Shoemaker on patrol.[127]

When he returned to Long Binh, Steve wrote one of the Americal soldiers suggesting that he serve as a kind of purchasing agent for the troops, since Steve had access to four very large post exchange (PX) stores. He asked the soldier, identified in his notes only as "Doug," to send him a list of items that he and his friends desired, but no money. However, Steve wrote that someone would have to take responsibility for collecting the money to pay for the items.

Steve wrote that he had been doing this for friends in the 5/7 First Cavalry, who seemed to want him to buy primarily instamatic film and mailing envelopes. He told Doug he would ship up to $20 worth of merchandise at a time. He remarked that he was making this offer to repay Bravo Company, 2/1, particularly the third platoon for the good time they had shown him while he was at Kham Duc.

To his parents, Steve wrote that he:

> took a short walk in the woods for a couple of days with a patrol—interesting and fun. I really do like to walk. And when you've got a pack on your back with everything you need to survive—from water and food to shelter—you just feel marvelously free—even if you happen to be tramping through some stupid old jungle or across some rain swollen river. (I've got some groovy photos of guys crossing the rivers, but unfortunately the moisture got into the film....)

---

[126] Notebook 22, entry of August 24.
[127] Notebook 27, entry of August 20.

The Cambodian hometowners proved an incredible success with the local papers in the world.[128] I sent out 38 and we have gotten back tear sheets (copies of the material as it appeared in print) from something like 15 papers, which is unheard of. The previous record is getting back two papers which used something and I dare say the whole office has not received back 30 tear sheets in the last 3 months...only one of the tear sheets have altered my story a bit—everyone else used the complete story as written and a couple used all 3 photos!!! Nothing like patting yourself on the back.

"The Fixer:" A Dust-Off Helicopter Crews' War

At Kham Duc, Steve spent a couple of days with a dust-off helicopter crew. He thought he got to know the crew members pretty well and thought them to be "good people with a lot of quiet guts." Steve flew on a helicopter named "The Fixer," by its crew, which was piloted by Army warrant officers, Terry Handley from Portland, Oregon and Robert Farrington, from Pittsburgh, Pennsylvania. The two other members of the crew were SP4 Claire Nelson, the crew chief, and SP4 Harold C. Gay, a medic from Wilson, North Carolina. Steve noted on August 16th, that there were incoming mortar rounds and AK 47(the standard Communist rifle) sniper fire around their hootches at Kham Duc the previous night.

Two days later, he noted that many of the American troops were contemptuous of the South Vietnamese Army. While accompanying the crew on a medical evacuation mission, he noted that, "Nelson, the crew chief, [was] vastly amused at the way I took notes when the hoist [of a wounded GI] was being made and we were being shot at."

Steve jotted down several impressions in his notes. He wrote that: 1) the North Vietnamese "really do refrain from firing on dust off birds—not all the time, but a good portion of the time;" 2) this AC (air crew) are in the dust off business because they honestly want to save lives. He noted their willingness to pick up wounded Communist soldiers as well as Americans. One commented to him that a wounded NVA soldier is a human being.

In late September, Steve sat down and wrote his first draft of article on the dust-off crew entitled, "The Fixer's Waiting War."

> Specialist Four Harold Gay is the Fixer's medic. He enlisted to fly but something went wrong and he ended up a medic. He volunteered to fly dust-off...

> Gay was shot down on his first solo in Vietnam as a dust-off medic. Here at Kham Duc, he reads a lot and sometimes wanders down to the perimeter at night and fires a couple of M-79 grenades to let off a bit of tension.

---

[128] US soldiers in Vietnam (who were "in-country") referred to the United States as "the world."

Specialist Four Claire Nelson is the crew chief, the Fixer's mechanic and maintenance man. He comes from Center City, Minnesota...

Misters Robert Farrington and Terry Handley are the Fixer's air commander and pilot. The mister comes with the rank of warrant officer but somehow in the context of the four-man crew, Bob or Terry or the phrase "your brother" seems more apt.

...Farrington is from Pittsburgh and picked up a degree in psychology from the University of Pittsburgh before coming into the Army....Their project of the day is to build Handley a new sleeping position. With the help of Nelson and Gay, the necessary walls are constructed of earth-filled 105mm ammunition boxes and the steel roof plate is lowered into place.

Steve mentioned that this lazy day was interrupted by two minutes of incoming mortar fire.

At 4:30 p.m., the dust off radio clicks and everyone jumps. It is only a communications check. One of the men remarks, "it's getting pretty gross when you almost start to wish for someone to get hurt, but it is so monotonous."

Fifteen minutes later, the crew heard small arms fire and learned that seven GIs had been wounded, Steve continued,

The casualties are going to have to be hoisted out. This means hovering over the jungle as the jungle penetrator [a device manipulated by Gay—see photo] goes down and picks up each man. It is the worst kind of lift...if the enemy starts firing at the wounded man he's finished. If they start firing at you, you can't cut the cable.

...It is that kind of war—all day—nothing and now at 4:45 p.m. seven casualties; three platoons tied down.

***

Up from the jungle floor comes the words, "we've got four people on the ground here. The four are critical, I mean really bad."

"The Fixer" circled 200 feet above the jungle, then the crew saw an infantry platoon.

Gay is now standing outside the Fixer on its landing skids, guiding the jungle penetrator towards the jungle floor 150 feet below.

Steve described how the crew had to lower the penetrator four times, once for each wounded man.

> ...the last casualty aboard, Farrington breaks in on the radio with "lets get the _____ out of here, we took some fire"...on the first flight once the casualties were on board, there was no room for Gay. He flew back standing outside the chopper on the landing skid, attached only by a strap.

* * *

> The two medivac helicopters at Kham Duc alternate between flying dust off and back haul. Back haul is hauling the injured men from the Kham Duc aid station where they are first brought, to the hospital in the rear.

Steve mentioned that flying back haul had the advantage of increasing the crew's number of flying hours and giving them an opportunity to take a shower, get clean clothes and their mail at Chu Lai, the Americal Division's headquarters.

In a second draft of his article, Steve described how crew chief Nelson had to pull the wounded soldiers out of the hoist and drag them across the helicopter—often unavoidably inflicting a great deal on pain for men who were already extremely uncomfortable.

In a spiral notebook that Steve employed to write down information and as a diary, he noted that "'The Fixer's Waiting War' died an ignominious death." Although conceding that the dust-off crews used the term, his superiors didn't like Steve's use of the term "back haul" because they deemed it too impersonal. They also found objectionable his description of the way Specialist Gay rode on the helicopter's skid, because it was a violation of Army safety rules. Finally, they deemed that Steve had overplayed the theme of monotony, and found objectionable his suggestion that the crew wished for casualties so they would have something to do.

Monotony is a relative thing. Seventy-eight American soldiers were killed in Vietnam during the first week of August 1970. This is more than the half the number of soldiers in killed in action during the entire course of the Persian Gulf War of 1991. From the Steve's papers, it appears that "The Fixer's Waiting War" was never published.

On October 20, 1970, almost exactly two months after Steve left them, Terry Handley and Harold Gay were killed when the helicopter they were flying collided with another. They were lifting wounded GIs out of a "hot" landing zone, (one that was under fire). Twelve soldiers died in the incident. There is no indication in Steve's papers that he was aware of their deaths. Harold Gay was 19; CW2 Handley was 20.[129]

---

[129] My sources of information regarding the deaths of Terry Handley and Harold Gay are the Vietnam Veterans Memorial Wall website and a website called "The Virtual Wall." In a memorial note posted on the Memorial Wall website, Dr. Herb Hamel, who served with him at Duc Pho, recalled that Handley loved medicine and looked like he was only 14 years old. On the Virtual Wall, a former comrade, Patrick Hayes

Back at Long Binh during the last days of August, Steve was confronted by the annoyances of garrison life. He was angered by being placed on bunker guard for 24 hours after just having come in from five days in the field.[130] Having pulled guard duty for the second time in five days, he wrote that he was going to try to get his company's guard roster straightened out. The roster, he believed, was a mess due to "some shenanigans." Without a reliable guard duty roster, he complained, it was impossible to plan his work schedule.

In his notebook journal, Steve recorded a conversation he had just had with his hootchmate, Sherman Carlson, a friend from Ft. Campbell. Carlson told Steve that he had known that Steve was getting orders to Vietnam before Steve knew. Carlson was so sure that Steve would not go to Vietnam, that he went to talk to their boss at Fort Campbell, Lt. Colonel Paul Lasker. Steve recalled in his notebook:

> ...Lasker and I got into the big discussion of V[ietnam] and it was because of his openness and sincerity that as soon as I learned next morning I was going to NAM, I rushed down to talk to L[asker]. We talked and he suggested some people on post here to talk to and he was in general just superb.
>
> I knew the moment I heard on the phone I was [coming] here that I would go for all my wanting not to go and all the crow I'd be forcing myself to eat but Lasker helped so much. And now 6 months later, I learn it was a neat little conspiracy, put together between Lasker and Sherman and that both of them had the modesty and good sense to let me think it all just happened.[131]

Steve marveled at the excellent mail service the combat troops received in the field. The Americal troops he had been with received mail every three – four days when supplies were brought in by helicopter. While he was with the Americal, one soldier received a two-quart canister of homemade cookies, which was greatly appreciated by his friends. Then Steve observed:

> Right now a lot of the line kids really feel kind of forgotten. All they read about is how the war is essentially over, how troop withdrawals are taking place and how casualties are down. And all they see is the same old grim business of their buddies getting killed.
>
> As one of the kids said in a poem he composed on his 21st birthday in early August while on patrol, 'all this soldier asks is please remember me.' ...I was thinking...perhaps some people in the church or elsewhere might

---

posted a photograph of Handley at his graduation from flight school in August 1969. He noted that everyone called Handley "The Kid" because he looked so incredibly young.

[130] Notebook 10, August 28, 1970.

[131] Notebook 10, August 28, p. 15.

be interested in adopting a grunt over here in the boonies of Nam. By adopting him, I mean every now and again they'd send him a care package of home made brownies or cookies or some such [thing] just to let him know that he is really not totally forgotten.

On September 14, Steve wrote his parents that he was busy working on his "hometowners" of Americal Division soldiers. He had mailed off 44 stories with photos already. He was very concerned about making a mistake and matching one soldier's photograph with another's soldier's story and personal information. To avoid making a mistake, he checked over each photo, his story and his notes ten times. He also went to the USARV office that kept track of casualties, "to see if any have been killed since I left. It is grim but all were o.k. this time."[132]

The week before Steve had gone to Saigon to visit several of his friends.

[I] figured after all, I'm the one that got them the jobs, so I might as well at least impinge on their hospitality.

I got a ride down with a Lt. Colonel. We had a marvelous no-holds barred debate on the US in Nam until the traffic got too bad in Saigon and he had to watch where he was going. He is a surgeon (neuro-type).
Spent most of the afternoon visiting with Dennis James from Ft. Campbell... visited Steve Styck also from Campbell—another happy customer of Warner's Nam placement service.

Steve also stopped by the Australian embassy in Saigon to seek assistance for his planned trip to New Guinea. He received very little help and was told that Australia tried to discourage visitors from going to New Guinea. To his parents, he remarked:

No sweat, I'll get there and have a blast and buy my $5000 worth of primitive art and resell it in New York for 15 g[rand] or so....

Finally, he asked his parents to send him a copy of the recently published memoirs of Albert Speer, Hitler's favorite architect, who was the Nazi armaments minister during the last few years of World War II. Steve noted that the reviews of the book "are incredibly favorable."[133]

---

[132] Although Steve did not say so, I infer that if a soldier had been killed, the "hometowner" would not be mailed to his local newspaper and family.

[133] Speer was released from prison in 1966 after serving a 20 year sentence imposed by the International War Crimes Tribunal in Nuremberg. After his release he wrote two very popular memoirs. There are many who believe that Speer deserved execution and was able to hoodwink the tribunal with his obvious intelligence and feigned contriteness. Some anti-war activists drew parallels between the United States' prosecution of the War in Vietnam and the behavior of Germans during World War II—particularly with regard to incidents such as Mylai.

On September 14, Steve was able to report to his parents that he would be able to go on leave to Japan. Then he filled them in of his recent activities, including a reunion with a friend from the lst Air Cavalry in Cambodia:

> It's been a hectic, but great week. After I got back from visiting Dennis and Steve in Saigon on Tuesday afternoon, I set to work mailing out the final 100 plus envelopes of photos of the Americal kids, i.e., the ones for the parents, wives, financees and girl friends. A monumental bore and pain in the neck but it is worth it . So I'm doing this Wednesday when who should walk into my office but Sundance....

> ...he is a 5/7 friend, i.e., FSB Neil—Cambodia type. In college [he was] studying to be an architect when Uncle [Sam] invited him to join the colors for two years as a grunt. [He] came over in January, [was] hit in May, been shamming, getting operated on, etc., since then. Now very short (80 days)[134]and working like hell to keep from being sent back to the field. Short people are nervous people and have a great propensity [for] getting killed in the field....

> [I] took him down to MACV (i.e., super US Vietnam headquarters, where [General Creighton] Abrams, etc., are). Borrowed a uniform from one friend, got him a pair of my spit shined boots, borrowed some orders from someone else and presto—instant REMF (Rear echelon mother fucker).[135]

Also during this week, Steve's supervisor, Cpt. Edward Cashman, sent him on an errand to the lst Cavalry's headquarters at Phuoc Vinh:

> The real benie [benefit] of the trip was [that] I managed to procure copies of about 80% of the Cav Division's weekly paper since the beginning of '68. I doubt if you folks realize the importance of this, but division papers are one of the best primary sources in existence. The WW II ones are worth their weight in gold to scholars and [are] rare as hens' teeth.

> There probably are not half a dozen sets of the Cav paper for this period that are as complete as mine. Really [it] will be great for Gettysburg [College]. Some day [I] will have to try to do the same for other Divisions.

---

[134] Meaning that Sundance had only 80 days remaining in his Vietnam tour.

[135] The derisive name field troops had for soldiers with jobs in the rear. They were also sometimes sarcastically called "Base camp warriors," or for the privileged few stationed in Saigon, "Saigon warriors." GIs were not allowed to visit Saigon without a pass or orders specifically authorizing them to be there. The military police of the 716th MP battalion (the soldiers who, by the way, saved Saigon during the beginning of the 1968 Tet offensive) would occasionally check GIs in Saigon to see if they had the requisite authorization.

So you should receive a large box in a week or two with 100 plus Cav papers. Don't be surprised if I send it registered mail...it is super valuable (not in money but in scholarly value)."[136]

Steve closed this letter by telling his parents that the day after he left the Americal Division (August 25, 1970), a transport helicopter crashed killing 32 Americal soldiers and injuring others. He was initially afraid that the crash involved B company, whom he had visited—but it did not. He also asked his parents to send him a copy of Ernie Pyle's autobiography, "Brave Men."

On September 15, 1970, Steve went on leave for a week with two friends from his office to Japan, where he had a "super time." He spent three days in Kyoto at the home of the parents of Hajime "Jim" Taniguchi, whom Steve knew when Taniguchi was an exchange student at Gettysburg during 1967-68. Steve told his parents that he planned to return to Japan in the spring, when his tour in Vietnam ended. He reported that he bought:

> Vast quantities of photography stuff, a 105 (mm) and a 24 lens for my Pentax and a super duper underwater Nikon Camera...great for the jungle. No worry about the rain, tripping while crossing a river, etc.

> I've begun to get some feed back on the Kham Duc hometowners—9 so far. [I] hope to get another 10 or 15 at least...

Steve closed by asking his parents to order 200 boy scout mirrors and to take the money for them from his checking account. He also asked if they had found anyone interested in sending cookies to the field troops. Finally, he noted that he took $500 to Japan and returned with 15 cents.

October 1970: Fire Support Base Guinn

Steve did not write another letter home until October 30. He spent the last week of September and October 1-5 with an D (Delta) company, 2/8[137] of the First Cavalry Division operating due east of Saigon, near the South China Sea and the town of Ham Tan. His notebook[138] for this period contains much more detail and introspective observations than do his letters home. He was very flattered to be placed on guard duty at the battalion headquarters at FSB Guinn. He concluded, "I guess they must not consider me to [be] a fuck-up." Steve noted that the field troops were very proud of their long hair since it set them apart from the rear-echelon soldiers who were required to keep their hair short. However, the battalion generally required the "grunts" to get their hair cut within one hour of their arrival at the base camp. Steve then recounted a discussion he'd had several nights before.

---

[136] Many of these newspapers are in the Stephen Warner Collection at the Gettysburg College Library.

[137] Second Battalion, 8th Cavalry Regiment.

[138] Gettysburg Collection, Notebook 20.

A couple of nights ago I was in the EM club at Long Binh and ran into Tim McGovern and Mike Lund.[139] We got to talking and Tim got onto my spending "so much" time in the field. He said I was a fool. He could see doing it once, but only once. Beyond that it made no sense, since he feels he can get just as good a story from the guys when they are on the FSB.

I started to defend my walks by saying you can get a feel faster from humping with them that you can't get elsewhere. And then I hung it up and guess I told him the truth. I just plain love to walk with these guys.

You are free in a way you are free nowhere else or at least I have never been elsewhere....Besides if it's my time to die I can think of no group I'd prefer to die in the midst of than a group of 11Bs in the field.

They understand death's place. They bleed in their hearts but go on as if nothing happened.

Steve also recorded on October 2, his delight at his increasing ability to adapt to the life of the field soldier. He wrote:

Two proud moments yesterday. 1) _ picked up my pack as we were setting up and with obvious anger said--your pack is heavier than mine.
2) Everytime yesterday, I managed to swing my pack onto my back standing up-- it is a bit of a trick. In Cambodia I always had to sit down and slide, --most undignified.

Of course my pack may just be lighter [than it was in Cambodia] but I like to think I'm just a little more skilled.

Oh yes, no one uses air mattresses--too much noise. A poncho above, a poncho below, hard core all the way!

The hard core way of sleeping didn't particularly agree with Steve. He noted in his journal on October 5, that he was able to get very little sleep without an air mattress. One day he hiked two km (1.2 miles) with Delta company and only 30-40 minutes the next day to catch a helicopter back to FSB Guinn.

Steve left FSB Guinn on October 7. He thought his hootchmates at the base "are beginning to get tired of the extra body in the hootch. Four ammo boxes wide and seven men sleeping--not good. Also only five air mattresses. Thoughts and impressions on Guinn: D [Delta Company] has it good."

Different 11B companies have a different feeling. A 5/7 was melancholy, intelligencia. CO [commanding officer] was a former WP [West Pointer], my buddies were college men mostly and B 2/1 impression was youthful innocence.

---

[139] Two friends from Ft. Campbell.

D 2/8 so far just gives a feeling of being 11B, perhaps it's just the guys I'm with, but listen to them talk and you can see them 3 - 4 years ago in high school not giving a damn about their school work but gung ho on girls, sports and cars.[140]

In his October 30, 1970 letter home, Steve provided his family with this description of his travels:

It was a marvelous trip as usual. Three days of very moderate humping in the jungle, then about 7 on the battalion fire support base, i.e., the little temporary forts sprinkled throughout Vietnam. [These] are home to the battalions working the area, ala Fire Support Base Neil in Cambodia, etc. The area is super quiet and the guys are quite relaxed. I went without a photographer—doing my own hometowner shots, etc.

It is considerably more work doing it all yourself and a lot more tiring. [It is] well worth it because you can integrate into a group a lot further. There were 7 of us sleeping in one 12 foot wide, three foot high bunker at the FSB (and the roof leaked like mad)....I'm getting a superb education in all the different values and notions that make up the collective whole which is Mr. America—and I can't help but believe [that] whatever I end up doing it will be extremely valuable. Besides, it is a hell of a lot of fun.

...I came back from that trip and plunged into the story writing end. Get off my 50 hometowners in a record 5 days...on one day I worked from 6 a.m. until 1 a.m. the next morning and then from 10 a.m. that morning until 12:30 p.m. that night....

Had the standard hassles also. I wrote a really interesting story on my Kham Duc experience with the medical evacuation helicopter people. The story was a study of the choppers' crew of four and the tensions of waiting all day with nothing to do and then at 5:30 getting called to pull out 11 kids wounded and pinned down in an ambush. Well, it turned out pretty good. Sgt. Aycock, my sergeant boss liked it a lot. My Captain boss had doubts about page 3 but after an hour debate, agreed to let it stand if no one higher up said anything in their review.

My Lieutenant Colonel then read it and made no comment on page 3 but didn't like any of 3 quotes ("too strong") and suggested I play down the theme of the tensions just waiting...which, of course, was the whole story. So I got disgusted and junked the whole thing. I think I may try to resurrect it next week but man what a hassle.

After this assignment, Col. Mock, the PIO's commanding officer, asked Steve to train a new photographer, Roger Mattingly. Steve told his parents that he hoped to get some photography tips in return. Mattingly recalls:

---

[140] Notebook 20.

Steve picked me up as the new guy on the staff for his pet project. Steve was one of the smartest people I ever knew. He looked at the office and figured out that nobody really did much of anything. So his plan was to go out on a trip and produce more hometown news releases on a given trip than had ever been done before. In effect, he was going to set the record for productivity for the whole office. The theory being that having done this we would become the fair-haired boys of the office and we could pretty much do whatever we wanted after that. Or at least have our pick of assignments.

It worked, but we worked like dogs on that trip. I remember being called back to the mess tent after dark to shoot the second shift of cooks so we could add a few more names to the list. Steve interviewed and collected information to write the story while I took pictures of each member of the company to send to their home town newspapers. One story covered a whole company, but I had to take a picture of each person and keep the ID straight to process back at the office. It was a grueling trip but we did set the record and after that we could do no wrong in the eyes of the office staff. I think we did 200 guys in one day working from sun-up until it got too dark to see. Steve was a slave driver, but he was smart about it.

***

After that I saw him off and on. In particular I remember him going to Australia to collect aboriginal art to export back home to resell for a profit. God, what a wheeler dealer! He pointed out that the art work was non-taxable because it was art, but could be readily resold. There was nobody else working on that level in our age group.[141]

"Sundance": A Friend's Attempted Suicide

Steve chose to take Mattingly to his friends from Cambodia, the 5/7 1st Air Cavalry, then stationed seven miles from the Cambodian border, just 15 miles southeast of the site of FSB Neil.

...we got up there and I was greeted by the great news that Jerry Pickering (the guy working on a Ph.D. In Chemistry) has got a rear job on the fire support base working in the tactical operations center....

...one night Jerry came over... and told me they'd just got a message that Sundance[142] had just tried to kill himself with his M-16 rifle in the field... he'd

---

[141] April 9, 2002 e-mail from Roger Mattingly to the author. .
[142] I have omitted this soldier's given name to preserve his privacy and that of his family.

taken his M-16 rifle, held it an inch from his chest and fired. He missed his heart by about 1 inch, punctured a lung and removed a large hunk of his back.[143]

Somewhat earlier, on September 12, Steve, had recorded in his notebooks a biographical sketch of "Sundance."[144] He had been drafted in January 1969 after finishing 2 1/2 years at a junior college in Louisiana. Sundance was sent to Vietnam in December of that year, after attending NCO school. On May 18, 1970, Sundance was wounded in the leg in Cambodia. In July, his leg was operated on. In his September notes, Steve wrote that "Sundance" was doing everything to avoid a return to the field.

In September, "Sundance" had only 80 days left on his Vietnam tour and was trying to get a profile (a medical determination) that he was not fit to return to the field. He had found a job in the rear but was afraid his battalion would not allow him to accept it. "Sundance" expressed to Steve his disgust about the manner in which the 1st Cavalry Division had cheapened his combat service. Now he complained, that everyone with an 11-B MOS who had been in the Division for three months was authorized to wear the combat infantryman's badge.[145] Sundance said he had to wait until he actually had been in combat. He also complained about the relaxed standards for awarding the Bronze Star Medal.

From his conversation with "Sundance," Steve came to the conclusion that many career officers were desperate for contact with the enemy and "body counts"--even if it increased the risk of injury and death to their men. "Sundance" obviously was not allowed to accept the job in the rear and returned to the field. There he became one of hundreds of soldiers in Vietnam to try to kill himself. Three hundred eighty two succeeded.[146]

In a notebook entry dated October 19, 1970, Steve memorialized a discussion he had with Jerry Pickering and Roger Mattingly about war crimes:

Roger brought up the role of Viet War criminals and I broached the notion [that] the worst criminals were the people like myself who believed [that] to come to

---

[143] Gettysburg College collection, box 1, letter of October 30, 1970.

[144] Notebook 20.

[145] The Combat Infantryman's Badge (CIB) was in Vietnam, as well as in prior wars, one of the most coveted Army decorations. Stateside, it depicts a rifle horizontally with a laurel wreath set on a blue background. The CIB distinguished those who did the most dangerous fighting from those who didn't. Even those veterans who hated the War were generally proud of it--much more so than a purple heart. One of the cadre at Ft. Dix, who had both decorations, explained that the purple heart meant only that he had been in the wrong place at the wrong time. The standards for winning all decorations varied greatly and were probably less demanding as the level of combat decreased. There was a bronze star for service as well as one for valor (awarded with a "V" device). I was awarded the former largely for not embarrassing my commanding officer. In the latter years of the war there was a bit of a scandal as to the manner in which decorations for valor were awarded to several higher ranking officers, who in some cases had been nowhere near the action mentioned in their citation.

[146]http://www.archives.gov/research_room/research_topics/vietnam_war_casualty_lists/statistics.html #cause

Nam was morally wrong, and yet, still came because such was the expedient act. Roger, and more to the point, Jerry, said that was their boat too.

These people who had the moral hang-ups with the war and yet came anyway are the fellows who end up performing their jobs the best. Why [?] because inherently they are conscientious and work within the framework of society's norms. Their (our) reaction, when given a job is to do our best--I wonder where we would have fitted in the context of Germany in the 30s and 40s.

"C[conversion]" Day

While Steve was at FSB Guinn on October 7, the American military command executed one of its recurring, surprise "conversion days." Soldiers arriving in Vietnam surrendered all their U.S. currency (greenbacks) at the replacement depot. In return they were issued military payment certificates (MPC), which served as their currency while they were in Vietnam in the PX and in the service clubs. Although it was illegal for U.S. soldiers in Vietnam to possess greenbacks, one soldier in Steve's hootch was having greenbacks sent to him from the States and was trading them on the black market. Steve believed that it was only a matter of time before this soldier was caught. Steve was also afraid that Army criminal investigators would hold others in the hootch responsible, even though they were not involved in the endeavor.

For transactions on the Vietnamese economy, however, soldiers were supposed to exchange their MPC for Vietnamese piasters at U.S. military facilities at an official exchange rate. Many soldiers, if not most, ignored this regulation. If the official exchange rate, for example was 118 piasters for one dollar MPC, a soldier could get at least twice as many piasters or goods or services ("the black market rate"), by exchanging piasters with a Vietnamese citizen or by paying a Vietnamese with MPC. If the soldier was using greenbacks on the black market, the exchange rate was even more favorable.

The South Vietnamese Government had made it illegal for its citizens to possess American military payment certificates. This was done to curb inflation and protect the Vietnamese piaster. However, virtually every Vietnamese citizen, at least those with access to American troops, made every effort to exchange their piasters, whose market value only went down, for MPC.[147] To discourage this universal flouting of the law, the American military, on a recurring basis, issued a new series of MPC, which soldiers had to exchange for the old series. The fact that the conversion was to take place and when it was to take place was highly classified information. Thus, the conversion was accomplished suddenly and simultaneously all over Vietnam.

---

[147] The Vietnamese piaster was devalued 133 percent a few days prior to October 7, 1970. Another way the Saigon government tried to control inflation was by allowing the importation of consumer goods. One of the things that struck me the moment I arrived in Saigon was the fact that the city was awash in consumer items, which struck me as very strange for a nation supposedly fighting for its life. Two Japanese businessmen that I dealt with at the Procurement Agency repeatedly commented on this phenomena and compared it to the austerity that their nation endured during and after World War II. They both had some degree of contempt for the Vietnamese as a result.

Vietnamese citizens holding MPC were thus left with worthless pieces of paper, unless they could anticipate the conversion. Rumors about an imminent conversion day were rampant in the fall of 1970--at least in Saigon. At Long Binh, Steve believed a soldier working the base comptroller's office tipped people off about the imminent conversion for a fee.

Vietnamese who had access to American soldiers, tried to exchange their MPC for piasters --at bargain prices . This created a moral dilemma for at least some American soldiers, particularly the rear echelon troops, who were more likely to have personal contact with Vietnamese citizens. The imminent conversion provided many GIs with an opportunity to greatly enrich themselves. However, to do so was to an extent, undermining the war effort. Secondly, exchanging MPC with the Vietnamese greatly favored those Vietnamese citizens with access to GIs at the expense of those who did not. It thus was inconsistent with the notion that we were fighting for the liberty of all South Vietnamese, not just a privileged few.

On the other hand, in the rear areas and particularly in Saigon, GIs worked with, and many had become friendly with, Vietnamese nationals. These people were really desperate. If they were not able to exchange the old series of MPC for piasters, their currency savings would be wiped out. It was difficult indeed to inform a Vietnamese friend that you could not exchange MPC for them because of your personal convictions. My solution was to make the exchange at the official rate, obtaining much less in MPC then I was being offered, for my piasters. After a decent interval, those Vietnamese citizens who were able to do so, converted their piasters into the new series of MPC.

At FSB Guinn, helicopters arrived and representatives of the finance office collected the now worthless series of MPC from all the troops. However, the choppers did not bring the new series; the troops were merely issued receipts for what they turned in. Steve noted that until he was able to get back to Long Binh, he had absolutely no spending money.

In addition to getting the new series of MPC, Steve visited Sundance on his return to Long Binh:

> He...for a number of reasons I need not go into, had a nervous breakdown and unfortunately at the moment happened to be holding a loaded M-16. He had only 40 days left in the Army when it happened and yet the damn Army got him to sign a waiver yesterday agreeing to accept an unsuitability discharge. He was a bit depressed about it and it seems to me a raw deal. So I talked to the JAG (Judge Advocate General, i.e. the Army lawyers) fellows up here and it looks like with a bit of pressure, [Sundance] will get the honorable discharge he deserves.

In a notebook entry dated October 31, Steve noted that he brought "Sundance" a box of his belongings. His friend immediately went for his address list:

One night when we were drinking he put "head" beside all the names of his buddies who were heads.[148] He'd been terrified it would fall into the hands of the lifers and they'd try to hang these fellows.[149]

At one point he allowed how for a bit he wondered if I wasn't CID [Criminal Investigation Detachment]…if I might not have turned him in for pot or something.

Steve concluded later that "Sundance" had decided to give life another try. He then vented to his parents about Army bureaucracy and his Lt. Colonel (second in command at the PIO), with whom he was obviously not on the same wavelength. The Lt. Colonel had announced that there would be no off-post stories for November. Steve had been gathering individual photos of soldiers for a Thanksgiving Day essay about the simple things a soldier in the field is thankful for. He concluded that the Lt. Colonel would kill his story because the soldiers in the pictures didn't have shirts on.

Such utter stupidity. So I guess if necessary, I'll try [going] over his head to our full Bird [Col. Mock] in whom I've got more confidence—but frankly at the moment, I'm about fed up.

Steve had another reason to be angry and frustrated. Upon his return to Long Binh, he found:

A mass of memos the gist of which is that I was not recommended for E-5 [the rank of Specialist 5].

My first reaction is disbelief. My second - embarrassment. Third, disgust. Leafing through the deal I discovered the reason for not being recommended. I was "flippant and unprepared" at the [promotion] board.

Well I certainly did not take the whole affair that God awful solemn and I may [have] made some cracks, but well, it's the first time Stephen H. Warner,--the quiet sober dude, [has been] charged being flippant. I have a secret feeling that as time goes on I may become right proud of that rejection.[150]

Steve wrote home again on November 4, explaining that his parents hadn't been getting letters from him because he had been out of the office 2/3 of the time since August. He was somewhat concerned about the fact that his section at the PIO had just

---

[148] Marijuana users.

[149] Notebook 14.

[150] Given all the work Steve did for the PIO that was above and beyond the call of duty, I don't understand why Col. Mock did not try, or was unable to get a promotion for him. In writing home after being promoted to Specialist 5 in September, I told my parents that my boss, Cpt. Jay Herbst, had pushed hard to get me promoted at the first available opportunity and that my commanding officer, Col. Chester McKeen, had "put pressure on the people down at the personnel office." A week earlier I had written about sparring good naturedly with one of the officers on the promotion board. It could be that I was just luckier than Steve Warner with respect to the composition of my board.

gotten its 5th new chief in the last six months. Although Steve's first impressions were positive he expressed some anxiety about adjusting to his new boss' style.

He reported that he was thinking of going to Hong Kong in January on R & R with his friend from Ft. Campbell, Dennis James. Then he returned to the subject of his friend "Sundance":

> [He] is finally on the upswing for good. I've been visiting him every afternoon since I got back and really it was pretty gruesome for a while. I figured the name of the game was just to let him talk and me do the listening. Well, boy, sometimes I almost thought it'd be a good thing if he did just die. He was so incredibly down. A total collapse of any self-confidence...After you listen to this for an hour or more everyday for a week, you get kind of down yourself...

> But things are definitely up now. After a three, or was it a four-day hassle with the First Cav Division, I was able, with the aid of a USARV JAG [Judge Advocate General Corps] lawyer, I lassoed into helping me, to get [his] waiver revoked.

> The waiver essentially set [him] up for getting an other-than-honorable discharge, which is utterly ridiculous. Well it turned out [that] the fellow who had supposedly advised him on the waiver was also the guy who was pushing for his non-honorable discharge, which of course, made him unfit to have advised [him]....But it's corrected now and I must say I feel pretty damn proud.

> I've decided to stay in Long Binh for the rest of November. I really do need to catch my breath a bit.

Steve noted that Johnson & Johnson (his father's company) products were all over the 24th evacuation hospital where his friend was staying. He also reported that he was having second thoughts about his planned trip around the world:

> ...running around Nam talking to so many GIs has really psyched me to travel around the US a bit. There is such an incredible diversity in that crazy country— and I'd like to see a bit more of it.

Initially, Steve closed this letter with a discussion of his plans when he got out of the Army. He said he wanted to spend six – eight weeks in Japan and then "bum around" for five – six months before returning to Yale Law School. However, as a postscript, he weighed in on the returns from the 1970 congressional elections.

For Nixon-haters the best news was the President's failure to achieve his primary goal-Republican control of the U.S. Senate. Anti-war Democrat Albert Gore, Sr., went down to defeat in Tennessee and Democrat Joseph Tydings lost in Maryland. Nevertheless, the Democrats came out of the November 1970 election with 55 of the 100 seats. The President was heartened by the demise of New York Republican Senator

Charles Goodell, an outspoken opponent of the war. Conservative James L. Buckley defeated Goodell and Democrat Richard Ottinger in a three-way race.[151]

The Democrats also retained control of the House of Representatives by a margin of 255-180. Better yet for those who despised Richard Nixon, was the fact that opinion polls were indicating that the President might have a formidable challenge to re-election in 1972 from Maine Senator Edmund Muskie.[152]

> P.S., with some of the returns in it looks like Mr. Nixon's big political campaign push is going to Overall be a big flop. I AM SO HAPPY.[153]

> HE'S BEEN A DISGRACE. AP CARRIED A STORY WHICH REPORTED JUST PRIOR TO THE SO CALLED STONING INCIDENT IN CALIF. LAST WEEK. NIXON CLIMBED UP ON HIS CAR AND GAVE THE V SIGN AND THEN TURNED TO ONE OF HIS AIDES AND SAID "THAT'S WHAT THEY (the students gathered around) HATE TO SEE."

> IF SUCH AN ACT AND STATEMENT ARE NOT TOTALLY PROVOCATIVE, I DON'T KNOW WHAT IS. HE JUST LOVES TO MAKE THINGS SO NICE AND BLACK AND WHITE. WHILE I CAN'T AGREE WITH THE LEFT'S MAD BOMBINGS[154] I CAN CERTAINLY UNDERSTAND THE FRUSTRATION AND BITTERNESS THAT LEADS TO IT.

> NIXON [HAS] TRIED A BIG SMEAR CAMPAIGN AND I THINK IT AND HE STINK....

> ...ANOTHER BENEFIT OF BEING ABLE TO TRAVEL ALL OVER NAM...I'M BEGINNING TO GET A FEEL FOR WHAT MAKES PEOPLE TICK AND ALSO THE DIFFERENT MAINSTREAMS OF VALUES, ETC. THAT FLOAT THROUGH AMERICA....ON THE WHOLE, THE MORE PEOPLE I MEET AND TALK TO, THE MORE OPTIMISTIC IN GENERAL, I AM ABOUT THE HUMAN RACE.

---

[151] *The New York Times,* November 5, 1970.

[152] Muskie had been Hubert Humphrey's running mate in 1968. Responding to the 1970-71 polls, the Republican Party embarked upon a concerted effort to undermine Muskie's candidacy. The Maine Senator, who tried to walk a fine line on the issue of the Vietnam War, lost the 1972 nomination to Senator George McGovern, the only presidential candidate who made clear his intentions to get the U.S. out of the war immediately. Nixon operatives covertly did everything they could to assist McGovern, whom they viewed as a much less formidable opponent. They proved to be absolutely correct on this point. The Republicans in 1972 were able to paint McGovern as an unpatriotic radical, despite the fact that he had flown 35 combat missions over Nazi-occupied Europe. Muskie ended his public career as Secretary of State during the last year of the Carter administration.

[153] The capital letters are Steve Warner's, not the author's.

[154] There were several bombings in the United States by anti-war radicals. In one of the most notorious, a truck bomb was set off outside of an Army-funded research facility at the University of Wisconsin in Madison in August 1970, killing a 33 year-old physicist. Earlier, the selective service headquarters in Madison had been bombed.

MOST PEOPLE ARE KIND OF TIMID AND NOT TOO SELF-CONFIDENT, BUT THEY'VE GOT A PRETTY GOOD HUNK OF COMMON SENSE AND IF YOU GO ABOUT IT RIGHT, YOU CAN PRETTY WELL COUNT ON THEM ACTING RESPONSIBLY.

What a lot of garbage this letter has turned into....Oh, yes, the mirrors did come. The guys at [FSB] Snuffy were mucho appreciative.

Sometimes, I think I should become a social worker and in a sense I guess I will be [one] no matter what I go into.

On November 6, Steve reported that a new man in his office, Bruce Anderson, was working on a story about the use of hard drugs in Vietnam. Anderson related that his understanding was that death from drug overdoses amounted to about 25 percent of the deaths from combat in 1970, (1,000 as compared to 4,000). Steve thought there was a huge chasm in attitudes towards drug use between officers and enlisted men in Vietnam. The latter, he thought, believed the Army should give up its fight to prevent marijuana use.

Steve mused about his future in entries in his notebook on November 12:[155]

I guess I really do want to be a lawyer. I borrowed Jim Nelson's Yale Law Catalogue today. Estimated minimum expenses are [$] 4750 per year--to [$]10,000 for my two years. Is 60 hours at any place worth [$]10,000?

Bruce [Anderson] has been giving me a hard sell on dropping law for journalism. [He] says I have a knack for it and could do great. Today he showed me the [help] wanted page [for] *Editor and Publisher*. There were several job offers for reporters in the Midwest. Kachemak, Alaska--which sounds interesting.

I am or was tempted. What a way to get a taste of the Midwest--be a reporter on a small town paper. But then I've got to be my own boss and perhaps even more I want to help people and do it by making comprehensible the uncomprehensible. Could do it as well in journalism as law, but law gives you some added tools.

I picked up a copy of *The Graduate* when I was out with C 5/7. At the very beginning he leaves home to find real people and then returns in three weeks disgusted and lost. Well, I guess that is what it would be if I sort of jumped into the Midwestern bit. Perhaps, all I need to make law exciting is to stop looking at it with $ and start looking on how it can help people.[156]

Steve also recorded his impressions of a political discussion he had with his new section chief.

---

[155] Notebook 14.
[156] *Id.*

On election day, I and Col. Carroll [LTC. Robert A. Carroll] were chatting about how our respective teams were doing...He remarked he'd become more conservative in recent years-upset by the violence in the U.S.

It turns out that except for last summer when he took the University of Wisconsin journalism deal from [the Army] he's been outside the U.S. for the last 4 years.

Imagine if your only contact with the US in the last 4 years were in a summer course at U of W and that is when the bombings were on.

What a distorted view of America you would get...must add that he is vastly more liberal than Gatzka and perhaps than Mock but then he's only been in charge here a few weeks.

In a letter home the next day, November 13, Steve complained to his parents about the rising cost of Yale Law School and discussed the burgeoning problems of substance abuse among GIs in Vietnam:

I picked up a copy of the Yale Law School catalogue yesterday and was totally grossed out. The estimated total cost for a simple individual attending the law school for one year is $4750, which means roughly 10 grand for my remaining two years. What a ridiculous amount of money, especially when you don't have it and will have to borrow about two thirds--uncle should chip in the rest with the GI bill. What makes it worse is that I only find about four courses that really look exciting. [157]

Steve then turned his attention to the issue of substance abuse, noting "the Army went radical yesterday," when it announced all soldiers over the age of 21 could now buy liquor, regardless of rank. He speculated that the Army was easing up on the restrictions for purchasing liquor in order to discourage hard drug use.

With regards to drugs they are the in-crisis this month...about a week ago Mock gave us a big howdown on how bad the deal was. I believe 24, 28, 38 deaths from or related to hard drugs [occurred] in August, September [and] October. Well, we all talked . Several [staff members] made the liquor proposal. All agreed boredom [is] the key problem. Also, cut any links with attack on marijuana.

---

[157] The GI bill was far less generous to Vietnam Veterans than it had been for World War II veterans with regard to educational expenses. The Government paid 100 percent of the latter's educational expenses for as long as they went to school. As Steve's notes indicate, Vietnam Veterans typically had to come up with 2/3 of the money for school on their own. Moreover, the administration of the Veterans Administration left a lot to be desired. After returning to law school, I received my first GI bill check in late November, two months after school started. For those depending on the GI bill, the delay was a substantial hardship.

...John [a new photographer] is quite up on the drug mess at II Field Force. Hard drug problem really serious. [He] says it has got a lot more so in recent months, as he says no one has had anything to do since Cambodia.

Steve noted that some soldiers were put out when their officers issued an edict prohibiting sexual intercourse with the "hootch maids." He also recorded his impressions of a recent trip to the Cu Chi basecamp, west of Saigon, and the promotion board's decision not to promote him to the rank of Specialist 5. At Cu Chi, he was told of the brutal murder of one of the "donut dollies" by a soldier at the base.[158] The "donut dollies" were Red Cross employees who staffed the service clubs at the major bases. Eight of them died during the Vietnam War, most in airplane or vehicle crashes. Also, from his visit to Cu Chi, he gained the impression that a good percentage of American casualties in recent months were suffered from American mines.

With regard to the promotion board, he wrote: "I realize now that the promotion board was correct when they called me flippant. I've become flippant in my attitude towards a lot of stuff here [for] self-protection." Unless, he was able to laugh off the frustrations of Army life in Vietnam, Steve thought he would end up either having a nervous breakdown or give up and simply not give a damn. He cited as a recent frustration the loss of four negative strips by the film-processing laboratory. As a result, he would be able to send out only three hometowner profiles, instead of the ten he had anticipated.

Steve wrote his parents a long letter on November 18, into which he obviously put a lot of effort. At the top of the letter in large handwriting, he wrote, "WARNING – This really is a top notch letter. Newsy, a bit of dash in the writing—generally much better than normal—so do enjoy." In the margin he wrote, "Please save this letter for posterity."

It began curiously with a description of a party in his hootch. He got "excruciatingly drunk."

[The] last thing I remember before passing out was the two of us wrestling for fun in a mud filled ditch....I'm still cleaning mud out of my ears—but it was lots of fun.

He reported that he received a tear sheet from the Springfield, Massachusetts, Daily News with his story about the French-speaking soldier (Michael Fillion) and the Montagnard schoolteacher. Happily, Steve reported that the paper had used the whole story, including a photograph in which he appeared in the background.

---

[158] Virginia Kirsch was murdered at Cu Chi on August 16, 1970, http://grunt.space.swri.edu/womenkil/htm.

We got about the top third of a page solid. Not bad on a paper with 100,000 circulation. What I don't understand is they didn't use us until November.[159] All I can think of is the envelope got lost between Nam and Massachusetts....

Also while I'm bragging, I got a letter from some weaving and handicraft journal out of NYC (New York City). They're going to use my story on the Roman Catholic missionaries and their work with the Montagnards....Better yet, they are interested in more on [Montanyard] handicrafts and in publicizing that the stuff is for sale.

Next Steve mentioned that he got a letter from his friend "Sundance," who was recuperating from his self-inflicted wound in Japan. "[A]ll is well and looking up. Really was a bright letter." He also reported that "Jamie," (Jamie C. Thompson III, from Barrington, Illinois) another friend from the 5/7 1st Cavalry had come by to see him for the third time in less than two weeks. Jamie had dropped in on his way to Sydney, Australia, for R & R and on his return. A physician at FSB Snuffy had sent Jamie back to Long Binh for further treatment for wounds to his arm. He noted that "all the guys are getting super drops to go back to school....Nothing will make me happier than to put all my friends from Cambodia on airplanes and get them out of this damn country."[160]

Steve also reported that he had a new photographer working with him. This soldier had transferred from another unit and extended his tour in Vietnam so that he could get out of the Army when he returned to the United States. If you returned to the U.S. with more than five months left in your active duty obligation, you were assigned to a stateside post to finish out your commitment. However, if you had less than five months to go, your term of service ended upon your arrival home.

We are going to go together on a story concerning a self-help drug program over at a unit near here. [My photographer] has a lot of friends in it (some hooked) and it should be fascinating talking with them.

Nam gets more fascinating every day. Because there has been so little contact since Cambodia everyone is bored stiff. Results: drug usage, especially hard drugs, is skyrocketing...all of it is utterly fascinating as a mirror of American values, hang ups, etc...this is the greatest laboratory for studying America I can conceive of.

---

[159] A Daily News correspondent, Carol Murphy, contacted Mike Fillion's parents on November 6, 1970, enclosing Steve Warner's article and asking them for more information about their son's background prior to his being drafted. Murphy added these details to Steve 's story, which appeared on November 10. After serving in the infantry, much of it as a radio operator, Mike Fillion returned home to the United States in March 1971. He subsequently graduated from college and as of 2002 works as a chemist in western Massachusetts.

[160] A "drop" was an early return to the States before the end of a soldier's one-year tour of duty. In 1970 it most often corresponded to the decreasing numbers of troops still in Vietnam. This author's tour ended 21 days early. Some soldiers went home as much as 60 days early. This depended on authorized troop levels and in some cases personal considerations, such as the beginning of the school year. The incursion into Laos in late January 1971 resulted in smaller "drops" than had been the case just weeks before.

He then thanked his parents for sending him copies of Library of Congress material about Ernie Pyle. Steve mused, "man, what I give to be able to write about Nam, the way he wrote about World War II."

He then asked:

> Have you received the batch of [black and white] photo prints of GIs that I sent? I do hope that the Thanksgiving story gets used in the Stars and Stripes.[161] The guys in the field get a charge out of it. Some grunts saw the pictures in the office a few days back and went out of their minds, [they] wanted to buy copies...I can't charge them...so I had some printed up and gave them a pile (If the world were made up of grunts, I'd never make a million!)

Steve then gave his parents a list of things he wanted them to send him: bullion cubes, dehydrated soup ("the really good stuff"); "PRESWEETENED (this is super vital) Kool Aid...if the sugar has to be added, it is a pain and impossible for the field...Kool Aid makes even the raunchiest water taste good...."

> Did I ever tell you about the lemon sherbet...whenever I'm out in the woods and get hung up on my thirst and am generally feeling miserable...I start thinking about fresh frozen orange juice and Mom's lemon sherbet. So both of you be fully advised that the instant...I walk in the door, be it 110 degrees below zero or what not, I may ask for some lemon sherbet.

Steve reported that he would not be allowed to leave the Army in Vietnam at the end of his tour because General Abrams[162] had changed the rules on this matter. Therefore, he would try to get out of the Army in Hawaii and immediately fly to Japan and then on to New Guinea.

> New Guinea really intrigues me. This notion of picking up four or so grand worth of primitive art down there and then selling back east definitely could be cool. A groovy challenge, so preposterous on the surface that people are sure you're a fool—but I think a pretty good business risk.

> Besides I've decided that if you're going to make it big, you've got to go for broke. And after being in the Army, I've concluded that going broke wouldn't bug me too bad as long as it happened because I was trying something big.

> ...I've also decided that after upteen million years of schooling, I'd just grown bored with my routine. Perhaps, that's why the Army hasn't bugged me more. It is just so, so nice not to be a student. Other people play in high school and college, I'm just a little slow and waited until I got out or got outed.

---

[161] The Army newspaper for soldiers in Vietnam.
[162] General Creighton Abrams, who succeeded General William Westmoreland as commander of American forces in Vietnam in 1968.

The Night Ambush Patrol (Thanksgiving 1970)

On December 5, Steve gave his parents an account of his travels in late November, complete with descriptions as to where they could find the various places he visited on a map of South Vietnam. Although he didn't tell his parents, Steve and his photographer, Henry Eickhoff, had lobbied their superiors for permission to accompany an infantry unit on a night ambush. Steve argued that the chances of them being hurt were less than they were when he was in Cambodia or at Kham Duc. Also, he said that it was essential that he participate in an night ambush in order to write meaningfully about it.

In his journal of November 20, Steve noted:

Mock doesn't want Ike[163] and me to actually go out on an ambush.... So I wrote up a 5 point, 5 sentence memo on why we should go out. All in capitals with the key 2 or 3 words underlined. Really quite powerful.

I and Ike like my point # 3 best--"participation makes possible the questions whose answers are the gist of any great story."[164]

Mock's subordinate, Lt. Colonel Robert Carroll, however, encouraged Steve to go on the ambush. Steve noted in his notebook on November 23:[165]

Mock still doesn't want us going....At that I collapse on Carroll's sofa with a loud curse. Carroll looked up with a smile and said, "but he didn't give you a direct order and I doubt if you'd be court martialed if you went out." Carroll still thinks it would be a better story if we went out.

After leaving Lt. Colonel Carroll's office, Steve went to PIO guardroom to check out his M-16 rifle. Although it was to have been repaired six weeks previously, he found that it was missing its firing pin and was full of carbon.

Steve flew from Tan Son Nhut, outside of Saigon, to Pleiku in the Central Highlands. At Pleiku, Steve caught a flight to Landing Zone English on the coast, the headquarters of the 173rd Airborne Brigade. Steve stopped at the base's NCO club, where he learned that a soldier had been killed a few nights before at the enlisted men's club when somebody threw a fragmentation grenade inside. He also observed, "Not much to do at English. No TV. The thing of note is the steak house--where supposedly you can get any kind of steak you want."[166]

After the fact, Steve wrote his parents about the story he was preparing for *Army Digest*:

---

[163] Henry C. Eickhoff, a PIO photographer.
[164] Notebook 11, entry of November 20, 1970.
[165] Notebook 11, November 23.
[166] Id.

After a night at [LZ English], we hitchhiked down to another fire support base near the Sui Cai [River]. You hitchhike from base to base—the MPs [military police]…frown upon you hitchhiking on the open road—the area is pretty fair VC country. Of course, fellows do hitchhike on the road, but it ain't no go[od] idea.

At [FSB] Uplift, we met the little Colonel[167] in charge and he flew us out to a mini base on top of a 1400-foot mountain at the mouth of the Sui Cai Valley. Really groovy, on our right stretched the great coastal planes—one of the major rice producing areas of Nam with the glare of the coastal sandbars and the South China Sea in the distance. To our left stretched the Sui Cai Valley from one to two klicks [kilometers] wide and disappearing behind a 2500-foot mountain about 10 klicks to our west. The coastal plane literally ends in a matter of 500 feet and in a matter of one or two klicks, at the most, the land is transformed into mountains up to 2500 feet tall (maybe that's a bit of an exaggeration—but I doubt it).

Anyway, we spent the night on Washington, i.e., the little FS base. The top of the mountain has been flattened to make a base about 40 feet wide and 300 [feet] long. Marvelous time had by all. Oh yes, the base's purpose—they've got mortars, radar and the recording elements for sensing devices which are scattered through the valley. The sensing devices give off beeps when something walks near them, then the radar is zeroed in (it is accurate to a meter), checks out if it is human, and if it is, the mortars proceed to blow it away. All very effective. Besides VC and NVA, they've blown away a 6-man US infantry team…and two men of another US infantry element working in the valley. The elements reported their positions erroneously and paid a heavy price.

Steve wanted to spend all of Thanksgiving Day with an infantry company in the field, but couldn't get on a helicopter until 1 p.m. Therefore, he spent the morning at the fire support base.

The chaplain dropped in and gave us a Thanksgiving service—sort of stilted, but the place, the people and an awful lot to be thankful for made it worthwhile. Finally, the chopper came and we hopped up the Sui Cai about 10 klicks (oh, don't worry about the mortars blowing us up accidentally—we're out of their range.)

At Alpha Company [3rd battalion, 503rd infantry regiment, 173rd Airborne Brigade] we run into the chaplain again. His Thanksgiving spiel is completely different now. Instead of reading presidential proclamations and talking about the pilgrims, religious freedom and atheistic Communism, he tells about himself. How he nearly lost his wife 6 years ago while she was giving birth. Something had gone wrong in the 6th month of her pregnancy and the kid didn't get nearly as

---

[167] Probably LTC Jack Ferris, commander of the third battalion, 503rd infantry regiment, 173rd Airborne Brigade.

115

much food in the last 3 months…Consequently it was the proper length when born but weighed less than 3 lbs. Anyway, the kid and the mother both nearly died and the kid was going to be a moron, but suddenly 6 weeks later, just before Thanksgiving, the doctors told this fellow that both the kid and mother would recover—and now the kid is just like normal.

Anyway, all this is quite corny in a sense. Tear jerker stuff. And when you are sitting with 30 other fellows in the middle of a valley, which has been Charles' [Viet Cong territory] since God knows when—and when some of the guys are married and some are fathers, or soon to be fathers, and the rest someday to be fathers—all the cornyness comes off as noncornyness. All of it comes out just like if should—moving and making you think, etc. Something like Country & Western music (the words are corny as hell, and yet, here in Nam at least, it's my favorite type of music because it speaks of the super simple, but basic things, with a straight forward innocent naiveté—which it quite refreshing (Lordy, lordy, lordy, what a paragraph !!!!)

Anyway, I guess I might as well tell you what our assignment was. We were doing a story on night ambushes—now relax, night ambushes are not as detrimental to one's health as you might imagine,[168] besides, I natch [naturally] volunteered for the assignment (no one else in our dumb office would want it anyway). So, after the services, we, Ike (my photo man, the one I used in Cambodia, also) and I split up and each joined an element.

…The company was working in 6 to 8-man elements. That night after dark, the whole company headed off across rice paddies and two damn rivers, all in utter darkness on Charlie Cong's trails. It was so dark that my nose kept bumping into the pack of the fellow in front of me—and this is when we are out in the open, walking through abandoned rice paddies. We spent the night sleeping on abandoned rice paddy dikes, simply wrapped in ponchos (it rains but I stay fairly dry). About 5:30 the next morning, I heard some noise so I tuck my head out from under my poncho. A shadow was standing over me and I asked him if it was time to get up. He sort of jumped back and said, "golly, I'm glad you said something, I was getting ready to piss on you…." I later learned that another fellow tried to wake up the M-60 machine gun…Waffles, the machine gunner, had covered his gun with his poncho and its silhouette looked [similar] to one of us sleeping.

The troops started moving just before dawn. The company was to patrol the head of one spur of the Sui Cai valley, which was ½ km wide and featured a 40-foot wide, four-foot deep, fast-moving stream. The objective of the patrol was to ambush Viet Cong soldiers on their trails. However there was no contact with the enemy.

---

[168] Author's note: One might read Tim O'Brien's *The Things They Carried* for a contrary view. O'Brien is the Ambrose Bierce of the Vietnam War. Like Bierce, who experienced the Civil War battle of Chickamauga, O'Brien strips away the euphemisms from war and leaves only the horror and gruesomeness.

It rained the whole 3 days...Charles [the VC] sat under his ponchos trying to keep dry and we did the same. No one bothered to ambush or be ambushed by anyone—we were all too busy battling the rain, the mud and the crud.

In his notebook, Steve noted on November 30:

[For] the last 36 or so hours, it has rained constantly--I and everything I possess are soaked, except by some miracle so far, half my T-shirt which I have on...several, i.e., most of the fellows are running out of water and so have begun draining the puddles which accumulated in the ponchos into their canteen cups...

Steve got to know the soldiers in his eight-man element fairly well and thought he learned much from them about night ambushes. He took 400 photographs with his camera (an Asahi Pentax), but found that his light meter was useless in the jungle. He was proud of himself for learning to switch lenses while walking. Steve found the 173rd troops, who had all volunteered for airborne training, to be different from those he encountered in the First Cavalry.

...I expected that this would result in a bit different type of grunt from the lst Cav standard draftee. I wasn't disappointed. Four of my Eight men came into the Army as the alternative to going to court and probably to jail. The fellows were a bit more violence-oriented and were considerably, no vastly, more gung ho than the Cav fellows. They like the night ambush bit working in small groups. They enjoy trying to outsmart Charles.

Yet, they are not blood dripping killers by a long shot. They have infinite respect for the NVA. They are awed by the fact that many [of the NVA] seem to be college graduates. [This they know] from the intelligence read back on stuff they take off the bodies, they consider [believe that] he has vastly more courage than they do—and are infinitely happy he has no air power, because they are certain he would have won if he did.[169]

Steve noted that he found all eight men in his element to be interesting people and liked all of them. He continued:

So for 5 days we got soaked and then we all came in on choppers and we came home to Long Binh. I might add that Alpha had been out 21 days and the kids' feet were disastrous. Immersion foot and ringworm are both major problems. Some of the guys were really hurting on the walk to the pick-up point.

---

[169] Author's note: It's unclear how many soldiers Steve Warner talked to about the NVA. In contrast, I recall in 1969 at Ft. Gordon, asking Sgt. Peter Pastecki, an obviously intelligent and sensitive combat veteran (4th Infantry Division) if he ever thought about what the enemy soldiers were thinking. Pastecki answered that he only thought about whether they were out there and wasn't really interested in anything else about them.

Finally, Steve mentioned that in going from the fire support base to Alpha Company's location, he managed to miss Thanksgiving dinner at both places. He only ate a 3-inch square of pumpkin pie that he found lying around at Alpha's position. However, he wrote, "it doesn't matter—there was nowhere I wanted to be more than in the field and I made it."

Steve's notes of his stay with the 173rd add some details missing from his letters home. He mentioned that the troops passed around copies of the Army newspaper *The Stars and Stripes* and copies of *The National Enquirer* until they were literally in rags. He found them both to be "really quite delightful and interesting light reading."

Two Thanksgiving services but no food--missed dinner both at FSB Washington and with Alpha Company. First damn time in my life I've missed turkey on Thanksgiving, but the fellows in Alpha still had some pumpkin pie left, so I did get a piece of that....

...the valley is really quite lovely, flat as a pancake, floor [surrounded by] hills or mini mountains up to 1500 feet..jutting up on all sides....

the lack of noise discipline is incredible...5:30 we start moving....As the dusk settles, the shirt sleeves come down and the mosquitoes come out. The platoon is assigned an area and then the Lieutenant assigns each squad to an area about 200 m[eters] and then the squad leader picks the exact spot....

He describes a stream the platoon crossed in the valley as being 2 1/2 - 3 feet deep, with slippery boulders. The soldiers crossed it at a 45 degree angle, going up stream.

Two GIs ask, ' where is your weapon? Have you lost your weapon?' 'No, I just carry a 45.' It always brings a look of amazement and a shake of the head.

He also commented in notes dated December 8:

I can't help but feel that part of the elan and spirit of the 173rd comes from that extra 60 or 70 [dollars] a month they get in jump pay...[the airborne mystique] is important for it continually is re-emphasizing to these men that they are something special, something that not every soldier is...This is the case even though everyone in the 173rd knows that the 173rders are doing exactly what the leg [non-airborne infantry] are doing...and that their airborne training is totally useless over here....

Steve made a few notes about some of the individuals he encountered in the 173rd. One, Staff Sergeant Michael L. Thomas from Las Vegas, was formerly a world champion rodeo rider. Steve found him to be a "real fine and smart fellow." Another, Sergeant Daniel J. Cervantes, from Montebello, California, had been a college student who had been drafted because he wasn't taking enough credit hours to graduate in time.

Another soldier told Steve he had volunteered instead of facing court action for failing to make alimony payments. Yet another told him that he was allowed to join the Army instead of being prosecuted for aggravated assault on another boy who was involved in traffic accident with him.

On December 2, 1970, Steve joined A Company for a party at the LZ English steak house. He noted that, "last time they tore down a wall." While at English, Steve had a discussion with one of the non-commissioned officers about legalizing marijuana use. The sergeant opined that when the Army removed its prohibitions on drinking and gambling, the incidence of these vices actually decreased. Steve wrote in his notebook:

> Must admit one of the things I've found interesting in Nam and even in the States is the remarkably little gambling you run across and very little on people gambling their months' pay, etc., also drinking is really controlled.[170]

Steve was rather upset at the news that the Army was initiating a prohibition against the wearing of bracelets. He considered his own a good luck charm. A few weeks later, he was similarly irritated at an order prohibiting the wearing of "boonie hats" at the USARV headquarters.[171]

In other notes, Steve commented on a conversation he had with his friend Jamie, from the First Air Cavalry. Jamie was working at Song Be putting his battalion re-enlistment files in order.

> To his surprise, he found that excluding the officers, there are no college graduates in his company--this surprises me too--however, he did say that there are about 20 kids with some college.

> These are the kids that really got caught. I suspect many are like Sundance and Cervantes in the 173rd, i.e., working and going to school at the same time and got a bit low on credit hours and were grabbed.

Steve also commented in these notes on the stories in the American press suggesting that the U.S. Army in Vietnam was not willing to fight anymore.

> The real issue is not that the GIs refuse to fight, even given the present pointlessness of fighting. Rather seldom, if ever, have non-professional soldiers been requested to go through as much physical agony to locate the enemy so they can fight him. To ask a GI to run around in the jungle for 20 or 30 days at a time in the hopes of finding the enemy is to ask a lot more of him than merely to fight an enemy which is sitting in front of him...

---

[170] Notebook 24, entry of December 2, 1970.

[171] Notebook 24, entry of December 2; Notebook 25, entry of December 21. The boonie hat had a flat top and brim all the way around it. The troops at headquarters had to wear the green baseball cap.

...The U.S. Army in Vietnam has in fact become a de facto occupation force. Put another way, the only thing wrong with the U.S. Army's morale in Vietnam is [that] there is not enough contact with the enemy, and a civilian conscript army not fighting is not doing what it was conscripted for.

Boredom may have been a major problem for the U.S. Army in Vietnam throughout most of 1970 and 1971. However, I doubt that most combat soldiers would have really wanted a return to the halcyon days of the spring of 1968 when there was constant contact with the enemy and 500 American soldiers were being killed every week. Indeed, I doubt that Steve Warner would have had the same kind of experiences accompanying field troops in 1968 or 1969 that he did in 1970. There is a good chance he would have seen action and possibly been killed in his very first forays into the bush.

The Public Information Office published Steve's story "Night Fighters of the 173d" on December 31, 1970, as a press release, with his byline.[172]

"We let 'Sir Charles' come to us," whispered the shadowy figure cradling an M-16 rifle and quietly blending with the concealing hedgerow.

For the shadow and its seven teammates, sitting in the dark and waiting for the enemy is a way of life. They are members of the 3d Battalion, 503d Infantry, 173 Airborne Brigade and the cause of the growing series of nightmares for the NVA and VC of Binh Dinh Province.

"Charles is a lot more dependent on ground travel than we are," remarked the 3d Battalion's commander Lieutenant Colonel Jack Ferris. "We just try to make sure every move costs him dearly."

The costs can indeed be exceedingly high as Charles has learned. One recent eight-man ambush team garnered 23 enemy dead, between 20 and 25 blood trails, two detainees, the components for more than a dozen complete B 40 rockets and 25 pounds of documents.

In planning the night ambush, team members had observed heavy traffic along the potential site all day. As darkness settled over the thickly wooded Coconut grove, the mosquitoes came out, sleeves were rolled down and the ambush team moved into position.

A dozen claymores [mines] were quickly implanted along the trail and linked with a detonator cord, assuring the enemy a scorching welcome.

And then the waiting began. For 10 hours there was nothing but the breeze in the palms, the chirp of the crickets and the occasional glow of a lightning bug.

---

[172] National Archives, Record Group 472.

At five the next morning the stillness broke as the hurried flip-flop of rubber tire sandals echoed off the trail and gradually a series of shadowy silhouettes emerged.

Claymores shattered the still of the early morning as 16 baseball grenades, lobbed into the chaos on the trail, added to the din. Caught unaware, the enemy frantically struggled to escape the holocaust only the find themselves pinned down by small arms and M-79 grenade fire.

Soon the firing stopped. Three ambushers cautiously emerged from the shadows and began to sweep the kill zone with more small arms and M-79 fire as they prepared to check out the bodies.[173]

Not every ambush is as spectacularly successful as this one but in the strategy of saturation ambushes, no one expects every try to be a winner.

"The name of the game is small unit action," remarked Lt. Col. Ferris. "We saturate an area we know they're in and then just wait."

With three or four companies each saturating an area known to have enemy movement with as many as 20 ambushes nightly, odds are excellent that someone will come up with a winning combination.

The crucial man in producing winning combinations is the ambush leader. Often a squad leader, he is the man who makes most of the decisions.

The battalion and company commanders can define each team's area of operations and if intelligence is sufficient, even designate the particular trails to be ambushed. Beyond that they can do little more than provide good team leaders.

Staff Sergeant Michael Thomas is such a man. Before he was drafted he attended college on a rodeo scholarship. Now he is an infantry squad leader and often in charge of night ambushes.

"On night ambushes you do whatever your imagination, the terrain and the weather will allow," said the native of Las Vegas, Nevada. "You can't use a detailed SCP because you set a pattern and if Charlie knows your pattern you're dead."

As team leader Sergeant Thomas is responsible for selecting ambush sites, determining the strategy to be used, setting up claymores and detonating the ambush at the optimum moment.

---

[173] This is obviously not an incident that Steve Warner personally observed. Rather it is an account related to him about an ambush that had occurred shortly before his visit to the 173rd.

Details which would be irrelevant in a larger group become vital. A bad cough is enough to disqualify a man for an ambush team. He could give away the ambush and get the entire team killed. Chronic snorers sleep next to guard positions so someone is always ready to wake the noisy sleeper the moment he begins to snore. Signals must be devised to instantly alert the team at the approach of the enemy. Even a route of escape, rendezvous point and password must be decided upon, just in case the ambush should turn disastrous.

Ambushes that Thomas and other team leaders set up are as varied and imaginative as the men themselves. Depending on terrain, vegetation, and the number of suspected enemy the ambushes may be commanded detonated, "mechanical," or a combination of the two.

The team leader's responsibilities do not end with the successful detonation of the ambush. After the area has fallen silent, enemy weapons must be collected and a quick, but thorough, search made of the dead.

Surprises are common. Documents stitched into a pair of black pants turned out to be an enemy roster and break-down of a vital code.

After a quick radio report the team leaves. At dawn they usually return for a more careful search of the area. Insertion of a tracking team and the battalion ambush critique team is then made if the situation dictates.

Mimeographed critiques, prepared by the battalion S-3 [operations officer], after an on-the-site inspection of each detonated ambush, are a crucial ingredient in the ambushes' continued success. Distributed throughout the battalion they serve as a constantly updated guide to what makes a successful ambush.

Critiques are studied by all ambush team members and not just team leaders. When there are only six or eight people, every man is vital.

Many men actually prefer their tiny teams to working in platoon or company size elements. Partially it is the knowledge that eight men travelling and working at night are much more difficult for the enemy to locate then eighty men traveling during the day. And partially it is because, as one soldier said, "the less people, the less chance for error."

But perhaps deeper reasons were voiced by Specialist Cecil D. Dunhard, a former Nashville, Tennessee carpenter and a veteran of numerous ambushes. "When you're in a company size element even the platoon leader often doesn't know what's up."

"Here in our team, everyone knows what's going on and pulls his share. It gives you a sense of pride and a feeling of accomplishment."

The ties of friendship flourish. Working and traveling solely at night, team members wile away the days in tiny camps, called laagers, hidden in the thick brush.

Laager life is low key and relaxed. Everyone soon comes to know practically everything about everybody. The men stretch their ponchos between trees and hang their hammocks or spread their bedrolls beneath, as daylight's hours are consumed in a seemingly endless round of talk, sleep, letter writing and concocting new menu combinations from C rations, dehydrated food packets and gifts from home.

But when dusk settles over [the] jungles and rice paddies the men set out once more to spend the night waiting for "Sir Charles."

On December 10, Steve reported to his parents that he opened their Christmas present, a copy of Albert Speer's memoirs, early. He said he found it fascinating particularly in light of the trials of the soldiers involved in the 1968 My Lai massacre and his own presence in Vietnam. He asked them to send him a copy of Telford Taylor's book, *Nuremberg and Vietnam—An American Tragedy.*[174]

In mid-December, Steve and six of his co-workers traveled to Saigon. There they had lunch at the home of their barracks maids in a South Vietnamese Army compound. The maids, "mama sans" to the troops, were married to career ARVN soldiers. Steve got a big laugh at the plight of one the men from the Public Information Office. This soldier got into a big argument with the driver of a cyclo (a three-wheeled motorized bike) over the price of his ride. The driver got so angry that he chased the GI down the street while throwing large stones at him. When the seven soldiers returned to the ARVN compound, Steve noticed that the soldier who had been chased was quite ill:

> I learned a little later why. Not only had he been chased all about but in the process he had swallowed a $100 greenback which he was planning to sell on the black market. He was afraid that due to all the commotion the MPs might search him.

> So now poor [name deleted] has a 100 dollar bill in his stomach and a very sick feeling in his wallet. I find the whole thing quite funny. I can't have much sympathy for [him] since the black market money operation ends up buying the explosives that have blown the legs off more than one fellow

---

[174] Taylor was the chief American prosecutor of Nazi war criminals at Nuremberg in the late 1940s, after Supreme Court Justice Robert Jackson returned home. In his book, he recounted the trial of the Japanese general, Tomoyuki Yamashita, who was executed by the United States in 1946, for atrocities committed by his troops in the Philippines. A no-fault standard of guilt was applied to Yamashita, i.e., that he was responsible for the crimes committed by his soldiers regardless of the fact that there was no evidence that he either ordered them or was even aware of them. Taylor suggested that General Westmoreland should be held to the same standard for what occurred at My Lai. Personally, I disagree with the theory espoused in the book and think that the Yamashita decision was wrong.

I've gotten to know in the field. But can you imagine swallowing a $100 bill.[175]

To his friend, Susan Walsky, he wrote of his plan to fly to New Guinea when he got out of the Army and then work his way across Asia on his way to England, where he planned to meet his parents. He mentioned wanting to stop in Japan, Hong Kong, Nepal, India, Iran and Istanbul, as well to ride on the Trans-Siberian Railway.

On December 22, Steve wrote his mother, asking her to send him a piece of the Montagnard cloth that he had sent home. He planned to give it to his friend from the First Cavalry, Jerry Pickering, who was leaving Vietnam in early January, so that Pickering could bring it to his wife as a gift.

At about this time, long before the Laos invasion, Steve started thinking about extending his tour in Vietnam. At a time when soldiers were getting "drops" of as much as 45 - 60 days, Steve proposed to Lieutenant Colonel Carroll that he would reject a drop if he could be assured that he would be allowed to travel at will.[176]Carroll agreed:

He asked me why I wanted to stay through March and I told him I had places to go and things to see--because at heart I'm a social and cultural historian and find Nam a fabulous laboratory to observe my generation.[177]

Carroll suggested that Steve extend his tour in Vietnam by six months. That way, he said, Steve could go to New Guinea on a 30-day leave. Steve found the suggestion appealing. He figured that such a strategy would be beneficial to him financially and would give him additional opportunities to write. For one thing, he thought that he'd have difficulty finding a job during the period between his discharge from the Army and his return to Yale. Secondly, this plan would greatly facilitate his trip to New Guinea and reduce its cost.

---

[175] Letter dated December 14, 1970 to Susan Walsky.

[176] At this point, it was conceivable that Steve could leave Vietnam as early as late January 1971.

[177] Notebook 25, entry of December 20, 1970.

Christmas 1970 at FSB Green

Steve did not write home again for two weeks. On January 3, 1971, he told his parents that at the urging of his superiors, he went out to FSB Green, 60 miles North of Saigon to do more "hometowners." On December 24, Steve, his photographer and an assistant did 110 photos and stories, taking only a ½ hour break the whole day. Christmas morning, they did another 50. Steve and his photographer then flew out to the jungle to shoot more photos and eat Christmas dinner. They took along a little Christmas tree with a stocking on it. Each soldier posed, usually with his weapon, by the tree. For each picture, Steve prepared a "hometowner" entitled "Local Soldier's Jungle Christmas."

_____ celebrated Christmas deep in Vietnam's jungle.

Home this Christmas was Fire Support Base Green, a tiny cluster of sandbag bunkers, howitzers and dust located in a jungle clearing 60 miles north of Saigon.

Christmas began on the fire support base with an incredible proliferation of Christmas trees atop bunkers and gun pits as "Do not open until Christmas packages" fell before recipients' curiosity.

Surprises never ceased.

One soldier received an assortment of musical instruments plus 100 sheets of Christmas music from a mother determined that he and his buddies should celebrate Christmas in style.

Another proud, if somewhat bewildered trooper, acquired a female mannequin's leg complete with nylon stocking and baby blue garter.

Christmas formally arrived at _____battalion at 6 p.m. Christmas Eve when the cease fire brought 24 hours of precious peace.

Soon after, around an altar formed of ammunition crates, men joined in a traditional Christmas Eve worship service.

Darkness found flickering candles and men clustered in small groups under the starlit sky to share delicacies from home, visit, listen to tapes and sing to the accompaniment of a harmonica or guitar.

Only the mess tents hummed with activity.

Between 6 p.m. and midnight, three cooks prepared and baked 84 mincemeat and apple pies and a thousand rolls as preparations for the Christmas dinner commenced. By noon Christmas day they and their 15 cohorts had accomplished the seemingly impossible: complete Christmas dinners including shrimp, roast turkey, two kinds of dressing and potatoes for approximately 500 hungry men.

Midst these activities, somehow the cooks found time to pack Christmas dinner for men in the field, prepare bag lunches for 135 individuals flying to Bob Hope's show[178] and cook and serve Christmas breakfast to 300.

Christmas Day was quiet on _____little base. Two Red Cross girls helicoptered in to distribute gifts and cheer. Major General George W. Putnam, Jr., Division Commander[179] and a Congressman paid visits. At noon everyone gathered for dinner.

The day was even quieter in the jungle. In dimly lit caverns hacked from bamboo underbrush, infantrymen gathered and ate Christmas dinners flown in by helicopters proclaiming "Peace To All Men" and "Merry Xmas Grunts" scrawled on their sides.

Suddenly the radio crackled, "Element 4 is in contact." Someone muttered, "Damn Charlie, tell him to cancel the contact, it's Christmas." As if in answer the radio replied, "Negative contact, be advised we think it was just a pig."

One trooper received his best Christmas present Dec. 26. Returning from the Bob Hope show, the surprised soldier learned he'd been given a 46-day drop and should be home in five days.

Not everyone could be as lucky, but_____ and the rest could at least share one young soldier's Christmas thought: "All I want for Christmas is my life, my wife and my home. Something I'll have next year, God willing."

---

[178] Hope brought an entertainment troupe to Vietnam every Christmas during the War. He was also very outspoken in his support for government policy in Vietnam and in his criticism of the anti-war movement.
[179] Commanding General of the First Air Cavalry Division.

After returning for a day to Long Binh to work on his stories, Steve flew down to Can Tho in the Mekong Delta, south of Saigon, to do a story on a combat helicopter company. He wrote his parents that:

> I've wanted to work with such a company ever since I came to Nam because these are the kids that to my mind are the real "killers of Nam" and I'm curious to know what type of kids they are.

The unit he flew with was Troop C, 16th Cavalry Squadron, 13th Aviation Battalion, 164th Aviation Group, 1st Aviation Brigade, under the command of Major Leslie Valouche. On December 31, 1970, during Steve's visit, the Troop, known by its callsign "Darkhorse," engaged the enemy. A New Year's Day release by the Public Information Office, reported the engagement as follows:

> Air crews from the 16th Air Cavalry, 13th Combat Aviation Battalion were in contact with enemy forces throughout the day yesterday in the U Minh forest in southern Military Region 4.

> The Darkhorses were conducting a morning visual reconnaissance in support of ARVN elements when contact was made. Action continued until the choppers were called back in observance of the New Year's ceasefire at 6 p.m. Gunship and light observation helicopter crews killed 16 Viet Cong.

In reports up the chain of command, Troop C reported that 3 of its helicopters were hit by enemy fire at 11:00 a.m.; eight more helicopter received fire at 1:00 p.m. Some of the reports described the incoming fire as intense.[180] Steve thoroughly enjoyed the experience of accompanying the squadron.

> Killing can be fun. I learned that today. If you're 18 or 19 killing can probably be the groviest fun you can imagine and that is the explanation of IV Corps' Flying Murderers.

> Confirmed CBA today 13, Col W figures probably really about double that but ARVNs refused to go in to check area...

> 3 or 4 slicks [personnel carrying helicopters] and all loaches [light observation helicopters] took bullets as did at least one Cobra [a helicopter gunship]

***

---

[180] MACV Form Dir. 381-34, Joint Services Antiaircraft Fire Incident and Damage Report for Troop C, December 31, 1970, Record Group 472, National Archives.

Killing the way the Cav does it is simply a very exciting and dangerous sport.

You have enough of an advantage to make the game worth playing and yet Charlie, though at a disadvantage, still can very definitely win any single hand.

The danger is always there but the challenge of killing without being killed makes it worthwhile. The key I think is the utter comfort in which you play the game, sitting in a chopper listening to AFVN--groving on some pop song and hunting for people to kill and then dropping concussion and incendiaries on hootches and watching them burst into flames, and seeing people down below and chasing them, trying to find them to kill, etc.[181]

One of the officers of Troop C explained to Steve, their rules of engagement:

[this] area is a free fire zone--we can kill any eligible male.

However, the officer said that usually the helicopter crews waited for signs of hostile action and never fired at women and children--unless they were fired upon.

While Steve was with the group, some South Vietnamese government soldiers shot at the American helicopters, apparently for sport. They seriously wounded an American crewman, crew chief SP4 Ted Rice. The next day the American helicopters attacked the ARVNs.

On January 2, 1971, Steve noted in his journal:

Talking to Ike [his photographer Henry Eickhoff] at the Binh Thuy AF NCO club. Ike: tired physically and mentally--became totally insensitive--didn't feel anything when they stuck 9 shot-up ARVNs on his chopper. It's true, except for Rice, I haven't felt anything since I got down here in the way of human compassion…Hopefully, a lot of the lack of feeling is caused just by the mechanics of the operation--it's all so impersonal.

After spending a few days with the helicopter assault company, Steve returned to Long Binh for a few days and then went on leave to Sydney, Australia for a week. In Sydney, he hoped to investigate further how he could arrange his trip to New Guinea. Steve then planned to work two weeks and then go on R & R to Hong Kong with his friends Dennis James and Jim Sturdivant from Fort Campbell.

He noted that, "in the language of the war, I'm getting short—be home in less than 90 days. I hope you can take me." Steve warned his parents that he was "pretty jazzed up" and tended to use overly blunt language.

---

[181] Gettysburg Collection, Notebook 12, entry of December 31, 1970.

Frankly, at this point, I'm sort of scared about coming back. I just don't want to settle back into the old ho-hum; office, school, proper routine for a while. That's why I'm leaving the rest of 1971 wide open—don't know what I'm going to do but I just need some time.

Just before he left for Sydney, on January 7, 1971, Steve wrote a letter in which he expressed some views that empathized with the foot soldier to a degree, which possibly would have embarrassed him later in life:

I never thought I'd see the day when I came to Nam that I'd be unwilling to turn a fellow in for committing an atrocity if I were a witness. And yet that day [has] come. No My Lai size [atrocities] but little ones; the chopping off of ears, pushing a POW out of a chopper to loosen his buddies' tongues, the smashing of a baby against a tree, choppers strafing a village with rockets and mini gun fire (2000 rounds per minute per gun) because one sniper shot came from the village, dropping machine gun rounds from 2000 feet into a populated area because you're bored.

And yet when you've drunk beer with them, passed the bowl,[182] shared a poncho on a rain-drenched night, received and given water, split a lurp,[183] well, somehow, it just doesn't seem right to have them punished.

Perhaps the generals, yes, but not Johnny or Joe, at least not most of the time. Take a boy or a man, cut him off from everything he knows, drive him nearly crazy with boredom, have his buddies disintegrate before his eyes into 'five pounds of meat hanging from a branch,' give him ice cream when he kills a gook,[184] and [work] details when he comes in from the field, have his commander chant, body count, body count, a hundred different ways, a thousand times a day, and can you really punish Johnny when he kills the wrong creature.[185]

By this standard, even mass murder can be excused. The troops who murdered large numbers of unarmed civilians at My Lai, including old men, women and children, had just lost several popular members of their platoon to Communist mines before they participated in the atrocity.

---

[182] Possibly a reference to marijuana.

[183] Dehydrated food package

[184] A common pejorative used by American soldiers for all Vietnamese.

[185] Brutality in Vietnam was not limited to crimes committed against civilians or enemy soldiers. For instance, the PIO news report of January 27, 1971 included the murder of the 23 year-old commanding officer of Troop C, 1st squadron, 10th Cavalry Regiment, a 1968 graduate of West Point, by an enlisted man in his unit. The murder was apparently the result of racial tension. A number of American officers were the victims of "fragging" incidents, killed by one of their own soldiers with a hand grenade. According to the on line statistics of the National Archives and Records Administration (NARA), two hundred thirty four American soldiers in Vietnam were victims of intentional homicides. However, the brutality of American troops was at least matched and probably greatly exceeded by the NVA and Viet Cong, as well as by our South Vietnamese and South Korean allies.

Steve was smoking marijuana, as were most of the troops stationed in Vietnam in 1970-71.[186] He was very critical of statements made by the Defense Department that it would strictly enforce U.S. drug laws in Vietnam. He asked rhetorically, "is it wrong to try to escape this dump with a few quick puffs." Obviously, in some situations marijuana use could be very dangerous. Although denied by some of the survivors, there were allegations that GI's marijuana use was partially responsible for the Viet Cong's successful attack on Fire Support Base Mary Ann in March 1971 in which they killed over thirty GIs and wounded at least twice that number.

Finally, Steve expressed nostalgia about his tour, which in hindsight strikes one as very foreboding. However, it also indicates that he found something in Vietnam he found nowhere else outside his immediate family--intimacy with other human beings.

How can one get nostalgic about Nam? I don't know but I have. Do you know what it's like to be in the field with a dozen others and to know death could be in every next step. The cost of admission is fear, but the price almost seems worthwhile--for in the bargain you get brotherhood, yes brotherhood, you're so close--close like two five year-olds are close out alone in the dark...somehow knowing you'd do things for the other guy that you'd never do anywhere else. For me, it's knowing that if I am to die, I can't ask more than that it be among a bunch of grunts. Why? Because grunts are the ultimate in humanness....

And so you ask me how I can be an optimist about humanity...well its because I've walked with Johnny and Joe and I've laid my life in their hands and been richer for the experience.[187]

---

[186] E.g., Notebook 16, entry of June 19, 1970.
[187] Steve Warner letter of January 7, 1971, Box 1, Gettysburg Collection.

After his return from Sydney, Steve went North to I Corps and the DMZ for an assignment. While he was there, the South Vietnamese, with American air support, invaded Laos in an attempt to cut the NVA's supply line along the Ho Chi Minh trail. American ground troops moved west along route 9 to secure the ARVN's rear in the northwest corner of South Vietnam. Steve decided to join this push.

On January 28, Steve was at Dong Ha and met with Lt. Colonel Robert C. Osborne, the commanding officer of the Third Battalion, 5th Cavalry Regiment (3/5), First Brigade of the 5th Mechanized Infantry Division (a Division which called itself the "Red Devils").

As the result of this meeting, Steve wrote in his notebook:

He's putting me with TOC [tactical operations center] track tomorrow which is probably great--a bit safer and I'll be able to cover the whole operation.

Yesterday afternoon, sitting alone in the Red Devil paper office, I ...almost decided to hang it up and go back to Long Binh and Hong Kong--but then I decided I can get to Hong Kong any old time, which is certainly not true for _____[I assume Steve meant Laos].

So here I am and I'm glad. I'll see my contact I expect and all and all I'm glad. I'm going--it's history in the making and I think perhaps my view is as valid as most on the spot observers and perhaps it's a bit different too--

So here's to you Joe. I'm glad I can come along one last time![188]

Steve attended a briefing for battalion officers and took notes. The battalion's mission was to build a Burma Road. Col. Osborne said he wanted discipline "handled ruthlessly and mercilessly and I mean precisely that." He opined that this would be one of the last charges the unit would make for long time and wanted nothing held back. Finally, he told his officers that he wanted the troops to have clean fatigues once a week.

After the briefing, the battalion operations officer, a Major Bissell, introduced himself to Steve and took him over to the command center where Col. Osborne gave Steve a personal briefing. Osborne told Steve he generally hated the press and considered them "absolute prevaricators" of dark gray who editorialize all over the front page.

For that reason, the Colonel told Steve, he rejected Steve's first request to accompany the squadron. He changed his mind when he discovered that Steve was in the

---

[188] Gettysburg Collection, Notebook 13, entry of January 28, 1971.

Army and wrote for *Armour* magazine. Steve noted, "he and Bissell talk in terms of me staying 30 days, which would be superb."[189]

On January 30, Steve noted:

> This morning the Cav attacked. No massive barrage of fire power, just a thin line of tracked vehicles heading west across the ruggedly rolling grass land...
>
> Up ahead Charlie Cav and 16 dozers were hard at work. The punch bowl road isn't much to look at, just a couple of dozer blades wide...By night fall the Punch Bowl Road terminus is 5 km beyond the initial turn off of QL 9.

Steve drafted a letter to Colonel Mock on February 2:

> Sir:
>
> I really haven't gone AWOL or crazy. I stumbled into a huge operation including western I Corps (I expect Laos before things are done) and am hanging tight with 3/5 Cav (1/5 Inf (M))
>
> The unit is currently carving an incredible road over the punch bowl's east rim into western I Corp where it will join with a spur of QL 9 northwest of Khe Sanh.
>
> I hope the accompanying short stories and photos will be of some use to you. Conditions aren't the best for writing and I'll feel a lot better about pictures when I get my Pentax, 3 lenses, etc. that I requested 1/5 to send up. But hopefully the enclosed is of some use. (Believe me it is an exclusive. No one else is around or can be).
>
> Both the 3/5 Cav and the whole 1/5 are rather tight on the press so we have great potential for some fabulous exclusives over the next month or so.
>
> Until I hear otherwise I'll continue to send you stories and photos--
>
> We've got an incredible scoop in the making and I'll trust you to let me see it through.
>
> P.S. Of course, I'm not interested in Hong Kong or any sort of drop if you'll let me continue to work this project.

---

[189] *Id.*

Besides the stuff I'm sending you, I'm taking color [slides] and more notes which we can use for Army Digest, Armour, etc.

Hoping you'll have faith in me and let me deliver.

P.S. I've never had such a ball am in beautiful with Lt. Col. Osborne (who hates the press) and the whole squadron.[190]

On February 3, Steve recorded that the North Vietnamese had fired rockets at the column the day before. However, he thought that the soldiers believed that the worst danger had passed. Then he opined,

> ...perhaps the real heroes of the Punch Bowl road are the engineers. There are about 40, these are from A/7 [A Company, 7th Engineer Battalion] but under Captain George B. Shoener, they are accomplishing miracles--with three dozers and explosives.

In his last letter home, dated February 8, 1971, he wrote:

> ...I've changed plans again. I just happened to be up along the DMZ when the big push west began last week, and being bored, I've decided to go along for the ride. I'm working with a Cav unit (i.e., Sheridan tanks and armored personnel carriers and grunts) about 10 miles south of the [DMZ] We're building a road west at the moment, with I suspect bigger and better things to follow. I just flew down yesterday to Long Binh to deliver about 400 flicks [photos] I took and write a bit. Tomorrow, I'm back up North for the rest of the month.
>
> The point is [that] I won't be taking my drop, that is I'll be coming home about 21 March, instead of late February...
>
> ...Don't worry about me. I'm having a ball and believe it or not, the stuff I'm involved in isn't that dangerous...
>
> ...P.S. if the stuff begins to come before I get home make sure you claim the stuff is "ethnic value." The galleries people emphasized this is critical in the customs deal.

Steve returned to the office at Long Binh from I Corps when Lam Son 719 (or Dewey Canyon II) began. He turned down a 23-day drop (early return to the States) and cancelled his seven-day R & R trip to Hong Kong.[191] He then returned to Khe Sanh and wrote two more stories before his death on February 14.[192]

---

[190] Gettysburg Collection, Notebook 13.

[191] Record Group 472 in the National Archives contains orders dated February 9, 1971 adjusting Steve's date of departure from Vietnam to February 25. It also contains his letter of the same date requesting that

The last piece Steve wrote was a draft of an article entitled "The Culvert," written about the activities of Company A, 7th Engineer Battalion, the outfit he was travelling with when he was killed. In the article, he described how the troops were carving a road to supplement highway OL9 to provide improved access to Khe Sanh and points west. He described how the army combat engineers were cutting elaborate switchbacks down the face of a 500-foot ravine and up the other side.

The engineers brought several large culverts to bridge a mountain stream. The troops used two armored personnel carriers (APCs) and a bulldozer to drag the culverts into place. Then they pushed eight feet or dirt over the culverts, thus providing the surface for troops to cross the ravine. This task was probably completed on February 5.[193] Steve mentioned that infantry soldiers from the First Brigade, 5th Infantry Division were providing security in the area, which was reputed to be full of North Vietnamese bunkers.

---

he retain his original departure date of March 21, so that he could finish his project of covering the activities of the First Brigade of the Fifth Mechanized Infantry Division in Dewey Canyon II.

Steve's decision to cancel his R & R was mentioned by his colleague Richard Moore, in a letter to his wife on January 30, 1971, expressing admiration for Steve's dedication to his job.

[192] PIO news release dated April 9, 1971.

[193] Entry in Notebook 13 of the Gettysburg Collection.

Steve's death sent shockwaves through his office back at Long Binh. Most of the soldiers at the PIO had arrived in Vietnam after Wiley Hooks' death in May, thus this was the first time most of them had been confronted with the death of a colleague. Upon learning of Steve's death, Richard Moore in a letter to his wife wrote, "he felt a close affinity with the infantryman and the lives they lead and liked to be around them...He is a tough guy to describe because there was so much to him. He had a million plans for the future."[194]

From their conversations, Moore, who had been in Vietnam for just over two months, gleaned that although Steve planned to return to Yale Law School, he had no burning desire to practice law. Moore surmised that Steve planned to make his living in real estate and that he might have had plans to enter politics, if an opportunity to do so came his way.

Moore noted Steve's interest in Indian and Aboriginal artifacts and recounted that Steve had purchased $1000 worth of New Guinean masks, carvings and other items and had planned to sell them at a considerable profit. Steve had also conveyed a keen interest in architecture. Moore recalled Steve discussing what he considered the extremely ingenious design of the hootches at Long Binh, a subject Moore noted he had never given any thought to. It was Moore's impression that although Steve had given some thought to writing a book, "writing was not really that much of his bag."

Moore recalled that Steve always joked about how spastic he was. He described Steve as having a thin, loose-boned, narrow face with light hair and slightly protruding teeth. "...the last sort of person you would have ever expected to really groove on getting out with the grunts." However, Moore noted that Steve walked at a very fast pace and that the few times they were together, he had to strain to keep up with him.

Steve's closeness to his parents and his sister was another thing that struck Moore. He recalled that Steve received a Christmas stocking from his family and kept it up for weeks afterwards. The stocking contained a lot of individual packages and Steve told Moore that he opened one up whenever his morale was low.

The letter makes clear that Steve Warner was the superstar of the USARV Public Information Office. Moore mentioned that Steve did 180 hometowners on the First Air Cavalry troops, "a new world's record for one story." He wrote that Steve could be childish at times, and that one of his most common expressions was "okey doke." But, Moore said, "he was tremendously intelligent and I had more respect for him than anyone else in the office. He was dedicated."

---

[194] Richard Moore's letter of February 15, 1971 to his wife. Moore's letters are contained in a file folder in Box 5 of the Warner collection in the Special Collections Department of the Gettysburg College Library and are quoted with his permission.

Moore recalled that Steve had turned down a medal and that he was the only person in the office not to be promoted to Specialist 5, when he became eligible. As to the war, Moore noted that Steve was certain that the North Vietnamese would take over South Vietnam within a few years of the Americans' departure.[195] In a letter to wife written on February 16, Moore recalled that Steve told him that all the United States was trying to achieve in Vietnam at this point [1970-71] was a graceful exit and Moore asked rhetorically, "who wants to die for that?"

In another letter dated February 17, Moore reflected that Steve's "luck just damn well ran out. He pushed it too much." He thought that Steve might have again been "putting himself out on a limb as he had done before," but wrote that his understanding was that what Steve was doing at the time of his death [covering the road building operation] was not really that dangerous--particularly compared with going out with the night ambush patrol. However, Moore thought, "he may have used all his luck up in the previous 11 months when he knowingly put himself in danger." Moore and others noted that Steve wanted to cover GIs when they were in contact with the enemy on the ground before he left Vietnam.

Roger Mattingly, who worked with Steve as a photographer, recalls that, "he felt he lacked one important experience to make his stay complete. He had never been in a fire fight. Most people who were short were willing to hide in a bunker for the last few weeks to make sure they got out alive. Steve went back into the field looking for a fire fight. It cost him his life."[196]

Richard Moore's letters provide a rare contemporaneous third person view of Steve Warner before his death. On December 4, 1970, two days after he started working in the Public Information Office, Moore described Steve in a letter to his wife:

Steve Warner, our man in the field, returned today and he is nothing like I expected. He is a graduate of Princeton and was in law school at Harvard when drafted--or that is what I hear anyway.[197] [He is] from New Jersey [and] definitely not what I expected of a guy who is beating the bushes. Admirable quality and all, that's where the news is, but until I find out different, I will act on the assumption that the field is something to avoid.

The next day, Moore wrote commenting on the relative scarcity of combat operations in Vietnam since the Cambodian invasion.

...had supper with Steve Warner, the guy who really digs the bush. He is out there all the time, was in Cambodia, and yet has never been in a small arms fire fight in his 8-9 months here. And with the way things are going, even infantrymen will be saying the same thing.

---

[195] *Id.*

[196] E-mail from Roger Mattingly to the author, April 11, 2002.

[197] Moore obviously was misinformed by his colleagues. Steve lived near Princeton, but attended Gettysburg College and Yale Law School, rather than Harvard.

On December 26, Moore noted that Steve was going out into the field for the third time within a month. On January 3, 1971, his letter to wife went into great detail about Steve's activities and Moore's reaction to them. Moore began by trying to alleviate his wife's concerns for his safety by mentioning that there had been only one public information specialist killed in the five years the PIO had been operating. Referring although not by name to Wiley Hooks' death in May 1970, Moore wrote that he understood that Hooks died when the helicopter he was riding in failed to pull out of a dive, although he understood that nobody knew whether it had been hit by enemy fire or had experienced a mechanical failure. He then assured his wife:

> I would not go on a story where the people I was with would be really looking for contact. Like Warner going on his night ambush story with the 173rd Airborne Brigade. Those guys were gung ho, looking for VC and he went out with eight man patrols who went to likely areas for infiltrating VC. That is the sort of thing I will avoid. I will not say that I won't go on stories where the possibility of being shot exists, because that would preclude almost everything.

> ...

> Warner has gone out more than anyone in the history of the office and has steadily looked for contact and it was only last week that he saw any real action (the night patrols did not trap anyone in the 10 days he was with them). He finally saw action of sorts by flying with the 13th Combat Aviation Battalion, who fly around in choppers (mostly Cobras with a command and control helicopter that Warner spent most of his time with)...also "loaches" [light observation helicopters]...Anyway, he went with them and saw them kill about 13 VC, no Americans were hurt, although some choppers were hit, including his, and four were forced down...Not crashed only forced down.

Moore closed by assuring his wife that he wouldn't take any unnecessary chances. Noting that many GIs were killed by booby traps, he promised not to go on any patrols, but he said, he could not simply stay at Long Binh, even though, "I don't think this country [Vietnam] is worth my life by any means, especially since all I am doing is PR work for the Army."

Returning to this subject in a letter dated January 10, 1971, Moore admitted to his wife that nobody in his office was required to go out in the field. However, he told her that you couldn't really do your job if you stayed at Long Binh. Moreover, being able to travel freely provided him with a great opportunity to see some of Vietnam and gain a better understanding of what the U.S. Army was doing in the country. He also noted that the soldiers from the public information office had a much better opportunity than civilian correspondents to mingle with the field troops. Normally, commercial correspondents were accompanied by a junior officer, serving as an escort.[198] The field

---

[198] This point was also emphasized by Col. Alfred Mock in an oral history interview done at Gettysburg College in 1993.

soldier was much more likely to tell another GI, who was travelling alone, what was really on his mind, than a correspondent who had an officer with him lurking in the background.

The Commanding Officer of the Public Information Office, Col. Alfred Mock, put Steve in for a Posthumous Bronze Star with an Oak Leaf Cluster. In his recommendation for the award, Col. Mock recalled Steve's extraordinary devotion to his job and particularly noted how he had left his sickbed in early May 1970 to cover the invasion of Cambodia.[199]

A former Gettysburg classmate, when reading Steve's notebooks in the early 1990s, commented that, "knowing how idealistic Steve was, I found his transition to cynicism understandable yet disheartening." I would have to disagree with the characterization of Stephen Warner as a cynic at any point of his life. It does appear, however, that he allowed his empathy for the American combat soldier to obliterate his interest in, or compassion for the majority of Vietnamese, who wanted nothing more than to be left alone.

Steve was not alone in this regard. To many, if not most Americans, the welfare of the Vietnamese was almost irrelevant to the Vietnam War. At no time was this more evident than in the public reaction to the court martial of Lt. William Calley, a platoon leader in a company from the Americal Division. In March 1968, this company murdered at least 200 unarmed civilians, mostly women and children in the hamlet of Mylai.

On March 29, 1971, a court-martial jury of six military officers, five of whom were combat veterans of Vietnam, convicted Lt. Calley of the premeditated murder of 22 Vietnamese civilians. He was sentenced to life imprisonment at hard labor. The American public reacted to the verdict with an overwhelming outpouring of sympathy for Calley. He was lionized a hero, often ignoring the fact that he and his men had killed civilians, not combatants. A maudlin recording portraying Calley as a victim and set to the tune of "The Battle Hymn of the Republic" became an instant staple of many popular radio stations across the United States.

President Nixon immediately responded by removing Calley from prison and placing him under house arrest in his quarters. There Calley remained until he was paroled in 1974. Nixon was not the only politician pandering to the pro-Calley mood. Many others, including Georgia Governor Jimmy Carter, did so as well.

---

[199] The records regarding the award in the National Archives also indicate that Steve may have been promoted to Specialist Five posthumously, however, this may also be a clerical error on some of the documents. His personnel file maintained at the National Personnel Records Center in St. Louis does not reflect either a bronze star or the promotion.

Lam Son 719, the South Vietnamese invasion of Laos, was every bit the fiasco that ARVN operations had been back prior to the American build-up. A few days after crossing the Laotian border, South Vietnamese President Nguyen Van Thieu ordered his commanders to pull out of Laos as soon as they sustained 3,000 casualties. In a matter of weeks, the ARVN did so, some in a panic, a few hanging from the skids of American helicopters.

There is substantial evidence that the operation was only intended to insure that the Saigon regime would survive through the 1972 presidential election in the United States. Henry Kissinger in his memoir, *The White House Years,* notes that Nixon's Secretary of Defense, Melvin Laird, "backed the concept of cutting the Ho Chi Minh Trail, arguing that it could buy us at least a year…"[200] He doesn't bother to answer the obvious question of what would happen after that year, when virtually no American troops remained in South Vietnam.

Kissinger writes that he eventually learned that, "four years earlier our Vietnam commander, General William Westmoreland had thought such an operation would require two corps of *American* [troops]. Though he was now a member of the Joint Chiefs of Staff, no such view was submitted to the White House in 1971."

Nixon is credited by Kissinger with, "the courage to face the reality that unless some steps were taken to interrupt the North Vietnamese buildup, the situation of South Vietnam in the next year would become precarious indeed." The omission of any prognosis for future years is telling. Nixon and Kissinger knew that South Vietnam could not survive without an indefinite commitment of American manpower and they knew that the patience of the American public for an end to the Vietnam War was not limitless.

As noted before, Lam Son 719/Dewey Canyon II was the last major American ground campaign of the Vietnam War. Casualties declined precipitously as a result. "Only" 1,380 Americans were killed in combat in 1971, ten percent of the number who died in 1968. About 150 of these were ground troops and helicopter crewmen killed during the Laos invasion. Three hundred died the next year. Still, there were a few dramatic tragedies remaining for the GIs in Vietnam.

As noted previously, on March 28, 1971, Communist sappers penetrated the defenses of FSB Mary Ann, killing 30 soldiers and wounding another 82. Alpha Company, 7th Engineers, the unit Steve Warner was with when he died, also experienced another tragedy. On May 21, 1971, a Communist rocket scored a direct hit on a bunker at a fire support base in Quang Tri Province, killing 29 soldiers, including seven of the A company engineers.

---

[200] Kissinger at page 995.

In Henry Kissinger's view, "the campaigns of 1970 [Cambodia] and 1971 [Laos] saved us in 1972."[201] He makes no claim that these operations materially enhanced South Vietnam's survival beyond the beginning of Nixon's next term. Indeed, he virtually concedes that Vietnamization was a fraud. Commenting on the failures of the Laos invasion, Kissinger observed:

> Above all, the South Vietnamese suffered from the flaws inherent in their military organization. They had few reserves; their tolerance for casualties was small, except for defensive battles.[202]

As it turned out the ARVN didn't have much of capacity to fight even defensive battles--on its own. It withstood the 1972 Communists' spring offensive only with the help of U.S. advisors, massive American bombing and helicopter support.

On February 21, 1972, Richard Nixon flew to Beijing to cement America's new policy of normalizing relations with Communist China, thus undercutting one of the primary justifications for the Vietnam War--the need to stop Chinese expansionism. Nevertheless, the war continued for another year. In October 1972, the United States dropped its insistence that North Vietnam withdraw its forces from the South. The Communists stopped insisting that Thieu be removed from power and agreed to return the American POWs. To placate Thieu, the U.S. unleashed a massive bombing campaign around Hanoi and the North Vietnamese port of Haiphong for eleven days in December, "the Christmas bombing." Twenty-six American planes, including fifteen B-52s were shot down--with over 60 casualties and 31 new POWs. Approximately 1,600 Vietnamese were killed in these air raids.

Peace talks between the Communists and the U.S. resumed in January 1973. One week after Richard Nixon was inaugurated for his second term, the final cease fire agreements were signed.[203] The last American troops left South Vietnam on March 29, 1973, and the last American prisoners of war were released a few days later. In his memoirs, one of Nixon's two principal aides, John Ehrlichman, recalled the following exchange he had with National Security Advisor Henry Kissinger.

> On January 23, [1973] the President announced the peace in a short, televised address. The next day I talked to Henry Kissinger briefly in the doorway of the Roosevelt Room. After congratulating him, I asked about the future: "How long do you figure the South Vietnamese can survive under this agreement?" I asked him. I expected Henry to give me some assurances. Instead he told me the truth, and it shook me badly.

> "I think," Henry said, "that if they're lucky they can hold out for a year and a half."[204]

---

[201] *The White House Years,* at p. 1009.

[202] *The White House Years,* at p. 1010.

[203] Ironically, the agreements were initialed the day after Lyndon Johnson died.

[204] Ehrlichman, *Witness to Power,* p. 316.

In December 1974, the North Vietnamese launched a new offensive. The South Vietnamese Army crumbled with a speed that astonished even those who held it in contempt. On April 30, 1975, the Communists entered Saigon and the war was over.

The end of the war, of course, was not the end of the agony for many Vietnamese. Over a million fled from their victorious Communist countrymen. Many left as "boat people" embarking on an incredibly hazardous journey, which in many cases ended in tragedy. An estimated 200,000 Vietnamese citizens were sent to "re-education camps" by the Communists.[205] There were executions in these camps, although not on the scale of the blood purges that followed the Communist victories in China and Cambodia. For that matter, the retribution that followed the Communist victory in Vietnam did not equal in ferocity that which followed the anti-Communist coup in Indonesia in 1965 after which somewhere between 250,000 and 750,000 Indonesian Communists and suspected Communists were murdered, and as many as 750,000 imprisoned.[206]

---

[205] On the other hand, there was plenty of brutality exhibited by the Saigon government towards its prisoners and opponents, often with the assistance or tacit approval of the United States government and military.

[206] Kai Bird, *The Color of Truth, supra,* at pp. 351-54. Seymour Topping in *Journey Between Two Chinas,* Harper & Row, New York, 1972, poignantly recalls the fate of one J.C. Jao, who worked for the Associated Press in Nanking before it was overrun by Communist troops. Although not particularly hostile to the victors, Jao was one of 376 "counterrevolutionaries" executed by a firing squad on May 5, 1951. The same day 293 people were similarly executed in Shanghai and 50 in Hangchow.

The Case That Can Be Made for the Vietnam War

The most legitimate case that can be made in defense of the Vietnam War is that the Communists are, or were, so much worse than our flawed allies, that it was morally, if not strategically, justifiable to prevent them from conquering South Vietnam by force. A decade before in Korea, over 50,000 American young men gave their lives to defend the freedom of the people of South Korea. The South Korean government also tended to be autocratic and flawed. Syngman Rhee, the leader of South Korea during the War had many of the unappealing attributes of Ngo Dinh Diem. Rhee was eventually overthrown by the South Korean military, which for decades maintained a corrupt dictatorship.

However, there can be little argument that the citizens of South Korea are a thousand times better off than they would have been had the United States not sent its soldiers to the Peninsula to stop the North Korean invasion. Although one can argue that Korea, given its proximity to Japan, has more strategic value than Vietnam, close analysis would lead to the conclusion that our Navy and Air Force would have prevented a united Communist Korea from threatening Japan anymore than Communist North Korea does today.

Whether the Korean War was worth the effort I think depends on whom you would ask. I venture to say that virtually every South Korean would think so. Somebody in the United States who lost a father, husband, brother or son in Korea, might have a different view.

The Korean War provides incredibly fertile ground for comparison with our Vietnam disaster. While there are some obvious differences between Korea and Vietnam, that these differences would be so decisive was not as apparent in 1965 as they are today. Many in the military believed that the improvements in American military technology, such as the mobility provided by helicopters, would cancel the relative advantages that the Vietnamese Communists enjoyed due to terrain, refuges in Laos and Cambodia and wide-spread support amongst the Vietnamese peasants.

Given the draconian collectivization of agriculture imposed on the peasantry in North and South Vietnam, it is not that ridiculous, without the benefit of hindsight, to believe that we could convince the Vietnamese peasants that the Communists were not their friends. If we had sufficiently cowed the Vietnamese Communists by 1968, as we did the North Koreans by 1953, Vietnam would be regarded as a bright spot in American history. There would not have been the social upheaval that followed the Tet offensive and the ripping apart of American society.

Even so, 20,000 Americans would have died in a war unnecessary to the defense of the United States, and many families of the American dead might still have preferred to have their sons alive than a free South Vietnam. Personally, I valued my life more than I valued the freedom of the people of South Vietnam. If confronted with a similar situation today, I would value the lives of my children more than the freedom of citizens of other countries that are not essential to the security of the United States.[207] I certainly valued my life more than I valued the objectives for which the war was fought after 1969. These objectives were the need to protect Richard Nixon's political flanks on the right and increasing the comfort level of the American people for the inevitable fall of the South Vietnamese government.[208]

A letter I wrote to my parents from Saigon on July 5, 1970, confirms that this has always been my view:

> ...I tried to ask myself why I am against the Vietnam War...I have noticed advertisements of a book by Joan Baez's husband [David Harris] who went to jail for three years rather than serve in the Army and have noticed articles about Captain Howard Levy who just finished 26 months in prison for refusing to train medics for Vietnam. What bothers me is that in the first great moral crisis of my generation I stood on the sidelines and let events play their course--hoping that when things settled down I'd be around. This is really what the majority of Germans did--hoped or made themselves believe that things weren't really so bad...
>
> I have justified my "participation" in the war on the grounds that I am not a conscientious objector in any sense of the word. I object to this war on purely political grounds rather than moral...The problem is that the more I think about it, the harder it is to separate the political aspects of my opposition to the Vietnam War and a feeling that something is wrong with this thing in a more universal sense.
>
> The thing about the Vietnam War that infuriates me the most has nothing to do with Vietnam, its people or its importance to the United States. It is how the U.S. Government has consistently lied, exaggerated and misled the American people to go along with the war. American society, once sold on the war, was unbelievably hypocritical in selecting those who would really fight it (and I'm not talking about myself).
>
> Once over here, I felt a little ashamed of myself--because like most everybody (Hawks and Doves) I had believed the Vietnamese not worth our efforts. I got to know a few and have actually become friendly with a few and now a slaughter of Vietnamese is as real to me as a slaughter of Americans...I don't think Americans can really think of these people as humans because most never met one. Even most GIs have contact with only the maid who washes his clothes and the bar girl who performs other

---

[207] I confess that I'm not sure I believe this in all situations. I still wonder whether the United States should have intervened to stop the Cambodian holocaust. On the other hand, I'm not sure how we could have done this without another costly Vietnam-like quagmire.

[208] Whether it was necessary or justifiable to sacrifice 20,000 American boys to maintain the United States' global credibility, as Richard Nixon often suggested, is beyond the scope of this book. However, I would not have wanted to give my life for such a nebulous concept.

services. Once Vietnamese become human beings it is a little harder to say let them stew in their own juice.

On the other hand, I think to myself there must be something we can do for them besides killing and maiming thousands of Americans and Vietnamese each year and making this country a cesspool of corruption.

In talking to Mr. Minh [a Vietnamese co-worker] I asked him how many people would miss political freedom if the Reds took over. He said very few--maybe 5%; what the South Vietnamese would miss is luxury goods-- which are much too prevalent for a country that is at war and has the standard of living that South Vietnam has. He said in Hanoi the people don't own Hondas and refrigerators--but then the streets aren't full of garbage either.

However, the city people like things the way they are and they don't want Communist austerity. If he is right that really isn't much to be fighting over--the South Vietnamese access to luxury items. If that's what the war is about, my sympathy is for the other side.

Minh also said...the Saigon Government has an awful lot of people who are in the government solely to convert American money to their own use and as a result has made little effort to win widespread popular support.

What I deduce from all of this is that there aren't that many people in this country who could not make their adjustments to a Communist regime if the other side won. Which to me means the risks inherent in forcing a coalition on the Saigon government are well worth taking. A coalition would probably be short-lived, but might very well provide a transition period in which the Communists could allow the die-hards to leave the country, while allowing the rest of the people an opportunity to adjust to coming events.

There is a lot to be said against the VC and Hanoi but I think within a few years they would have at least the passive support of the South Vietnamese people...in summary, I just can't see the point of fighting to preserve Vietnamese society as it exists today.

Acknowledgements

First and foremost my thanks goes to **David Hedrick** at the Musselman Library at Gettysburg College. As keeper of the Stephen H. Warner Collection in the Special Collections Department, David organized Steve's papers and put some of his photos and excerpts of his letters on the internet. Without his efforts, this book would have been utterly impossible.

Secondly, I would like to thank **Mrs. Esther Warner**, Steve's mother, and **Mrs. Victoria Warner**, Steve's sister, for providing me information on their family's background and Steve's youth, as well as some photographs.

Thirdly, I would like to thank **Karen Drickamer**, the current head of the Special Collections Department and her student staff, for all their assistance on my visits to Gettysburg College. .

Finally, I am greatly indebted to many friends and acquaintances of Steve Warner, as well as individuals who merely crossed paths with him in Vietnam. *Special thanks* are due to **Susan Walsky Gray** and **John Schiller**, close college friends for their assistance and to **Richard A. Moore**, who donated copies of his Vietnam letters to Gettysburg College. Moore's letters contain rare and invaluable observations about Steve before Moore knew what was going to happen to him. Others to whom I am indebted to are as follows:

Professor Roger Stemen (Gettysburg College)--who not only shared his recollections of Steve Warner but was kind enough to read a draft of my manuscript and offer many helpful suggestions.

Professor Charles Glatfelter (Gettysburg College)

Michael J. Hobor (friend of Steve Warner from Gettysburg College)

Sherman Carlson (friend of Steve Warner from Ft. Campbell and Long Binh)

Dennis James, Jr. (friend from Ft. Campbell)--who provided me with his recollections of Steve Warner and also reviewed a copy of this manuscript.

Michael Lund (friend from Ft. Campbell and Long Binh)

Timothy McGovern (friend from Long Binh)

Roger Mattingly (a PIO photographer in Vietnam)

Michael Fillion (A First Cavalry Division soldier profiled by Steve)

Alfonso Varela (a veteran of A Company, 7th Engineer battalion), who provided me with valuable insights about his unit and what it was doing in February 1971.

Lee McCain (Squad Leader A Company, 7th Engineers, February 1971)

George Baldwin, an A/7 veteran who maintains a website for his unit and led me to Varela and McCain, who were with the company on February 14, 1971.

Jeffrey L. Braun and **Jeffrey Orleans** for their recollections of Steve at Yale Law School.

Robert Giannasi and **Jeanne Elizabeth Jurgens** for proof reading my manuscript and offering numerous suggestions and a lot of encouragement.

I apologize if I have omitted anyone else.[209]

---

[209] I employed every strategy I could think of to try to contact "Sundance," Jerry Pickering and Jamie Thompson, Steve's friends from the 5/7, including calling several of the "wrong" Jerry Pickerings. I also tried very hard to find Henry Eickhoff, Steve's photographer on a number of his outings. Obviously, after the passage of thirty years, there is no guarantee that they are even still alive.

Notes on Sources

My primary source for this book is the Stephen H. Warner collection at the Musselman Library at Gettysburg College. Additionally, Susan Walsky Gray was gracious enough to provide me with copies of a number of letters she received from Steve Warner when he was at law school and in the Army. Another unpublished source is the letters that I wrote to my parents and sister between July 1969 and March 1971. These are neatly organized in a notebook in my basement due to the insistence of my wife, Susan. I also tried to contact as many people who knew or had contact with Steve Warner as possible. I have mentioned those who provided me with significant insights by letter, email or orally in my acknowledgements.

I relied heavily on *The New York Times* one of the few, if not the only newspaper which is effectively indexed for the Vietnam period.

Since my return from Vietnam, I have gone through several widely separated periods of intensive reading on the war. Some, but not necessarily all of the books, that have struck a particularly responsive chord with me are as follows: The *Best and The Brightest* by David Halberstam; *Fire in The Lake*, by Francis Fitzgerald; *A Bright and Shinning Lie*, by Neil Sheehan; *Rumor of War*, By Philip Caputo; *Chickenhawk* by Robert Mason, a helicopter pilot; *The Killing Zone*, by Frederick Downs; *Fortunate Son*, by Lewis Puller; *After Tet*, by Ronald Spector; *If I Die In a Combat Zone*, by Tim O'Brien--as well as his fictional works, *The Things They Carried* and *Going After Cacciato*.

Stanley Karnow's *Vietnam: A History* is a good starting point for reading about the Vietnam War. However, most Americans will want to skip or skim through his extensive coverage of the French experience. Karnow's book is also a little sparse with regard to the latter stages of the war. For this period, I would suggest Chapter 14 (pp. 569-614) of Tom Wicker's *One of Us: Richard Nixon and the American Dream* or Jeffrey Kimball's comprehensive book, *Nixon's Vietnam War*. Wicker's book is a very even-handed assessment of Richard Nixon, and at times surprisingly sympathetic. He gives Nixon the credit he deserves for one of the greatest foreign policy achievements in American History, the normalization of relations with Communist China. However, Wicker shares this author's critical views of Nixon's conduct of the Vietnam War and his penchant for nebulous concepts of geopolitical strategy that caused Nixon to undermine the democratically-elected socialist government in Chile and "tilt" towards Pakistan when the Indian Army invaded what is now Bangladesh and put an end to Pakistani genocide.

I am also deeply indebted to Lawrence Baskir and William Strauss for their compilation of information regarding manpower issues during the Vietnam War in *Chance and Circumstance*.

About the Author

Arthur Amchan grew up in Arlington, Virginia and graduated *magna cum laude* from Miami University, Oxford, Ohio in 1967. He attended Harvard Law School from 1967 to 1969 and then was drafted into the Army. Arthur did his basic training at Fort Dix, New Jersey during July and August 1969 as a member of B Company, 5th Battalion, 2nd Brigade. He was then assigned to the radio school at Fort Dix, where he spent seven weeks. In October 1969, Arthur was sent for more advanced training to the radio-teletype school at Fort Gordon, Georgia. There he was pulled out of the training cycle and made a company clerk in E Company, Eighth Battalion of the Signal School Brigade.

In January 1970, Arthur was "levied" to Vietnam. He reported to Ft. Lewis, Washington on March 26, and arrived at Cam Rahn Bay on April 10, 1970. After being sent to the 90th Replacement Battalion at Long Binh, Arthur was assigned to the U.S. Army Procurement Agency, which was located in Saigon, about a mile and a half from the Tan Son Nhut Air Force Base. During his tour, he made business trips to Tan An, Cu Chi, Tay Ninh, Dalat and Long Binh. He left Vietnam on March 15, 1971, returned to the Harvard Law School and graduated in 1972. Arthur has spent his professional career primarily in the fields of labor and occupational safety and health law. He is currently an administrative law judge with the National Labor Relations Board.

Arthur is married and has three children. Previously, he has written three historical books. The first, entitled *The Most Famous Soldier in America*, is a biography of Nelson A. Miles. Miles was a general in the Civil War at the age of 25, one of the Army's most successful Indian fighters and Commanding General of the U. S. Army during the Spanish American War and Philippine Insurrection.

Arthur's second book, *Heroes, Martyrs and Survivors of the Civil War*, consists of twenty-two biographical sketches of Civil War figures. Arthur's most recent book, *The Kaiser's Senator*, concerns Senator Robert M. LaFollette's opposition to American participation in World War I. He has also written *The Slower Runner's Guide*, a book for the talentless jogger and an article in the CCH Labor Law Journal regarding provisions in state workers compensation laws that prevent an injured employee from suing his or her employer in order to recover damages for injuries sustained due to the employer's negligence.